CHAUCER'S CONSTANCE
AND
ACCUSED QUEENS

CHAUCER'S CONSTANCE AND ACCUSED QUEENS

By
MARGARET SCHLAUCH, Ph.D.

Assistant Professor of English
in
New York University

THE NEW YORK UNIVERSITY PRESS
WASHINGTON SQUARE EAST, NEW YORK CITY
1927

Copyright 1927 by
NEW YORK UNIVERSITY

THE NEW YORK UNIVERSITY PRESS
ARTHUR HUNTINGTON NASON, PH.D., DIRECTOR

THE KENNEBEC JOURNAL PRESS
AUGUSTA, MAINE

PREFACE

ALTHOUGH several studies have been made of the immediate sources and analogues of Chaucer's *Man of Law's Tale*, that part of his story which treats of an accused and innocent queen exiled and restored, has not yet been considered in relation to all other families of stories containing this general formula. It is the purpose of my study to make this broader comparison, and to include also the märchen material about accused queens which contributes to the clearer understanding of Chaucer's Constance. I have used as secondary point of departure the Old Flemish play of *Esmoreit*, which contains elements of both folk-tale and romance, because it conveniently supplements the motifs to be found in Chaucer's story. The play has recently been brought to the attention of English readers in the translation by Professor Harry Morgan Ayres.

A great part of my investigation was made easier for me by the kindness and helpfulness of the staff of the Columbia University Library. Had I not, however, been enabled by a fellowship of the American Association of University Women to continue my study abroad, I could not have included a discussion of a number of unpublished versions inaccessible in America. It has been my privilege to work in the Staatsbibliothek of Munich, the University Library of Leiden, the Royal Library at The Hague, the British Museum, and the Bibliothèque Nationale in Paris. To the officials of these institutions, I am indebted for unfailing courtesy and helpfulness; to Professor Josef Schick of Munich for stimulating suggestions and advice. Professor A. J. Barnouw of Columbia University has given me invaluable assistance in the study of the medieval literature of the Netherlands, and particularly in the investigation of the *Esmoreit*-problem; and Professor Franz Boas very kindly clarified for me some of the vexed issues of modern anthropology. From Professor W. W. Lawrence of Columbia University, I have received assistance for which I am unable to express adequate thanks. His scholarly advice has shaped this work from the beginning, and his unwearied kindness has helped me through the arduous task of revising and correcting the text of the discussion. Finally, I am indebted to Professor George Lyman Kittredge of Harvard University, as reader for the New York University Press, for his constructive criticism of my manuscript; and to Professor Arthur H. Nason, Director, and Miss Hannah E. Steen, of the Press, for their editorial and typographical oversight of its publication.

The study now completed has been a delightful adventure to me; I trust that it may prove helpful to others who are interested in the literature of folk-tales and romance.

M.S.

New York City
January 19, 1927

CONTENTS

CHAPTER		PAGE
I.	Introductory	3
	Chaucer's Constance as an Accused Queen	
	The Queen in *Esmoreit* compared to Constance	
II.	Accused Queens in Folk-Tales........................	12
	A. The Accusation of Infanticide........................	12
	Infanticide in Märchen	
	Infanticide among Primitive People	
	B. The Accusation of Animal Birth....................	21
	Primitive Belief in Animal Birth	
	C. Motivation of the Persecution.........................	40
	The Father as Persecutor: evidence that he is a matriarchal ruler trying to prevent the succession of a son-in-law	
	The Mother-in-law as Persecutor: evidence that she is a matriarchal character	
	D. Other Märchen Types...................................	47
III.	The Accused Queen in Romance: Folk-Tale Survivals.....	62
	The Constance-cycle	
	The Swan Children cycle	
IV.	The Accused Queen in Romance *cont'd*: The Advent of the Villain	86
	The Octavian-cycle	
	The Valentine-cycle	
V.	The Accused Queen in Romance *cont'd*: The Villain as Sole Accuser	95
	A. The Ambitious Accuser...............................	95
	B. The Seneschal as Accuser............................	98
	C. The Lover and Dwarf as Accusers..................	104
	D. Persecutors in Pious Tales..........................	106
	E. The Brother-in-law as Accuser.....................	108
	Summary	113
Appendix I.	Additional Analogues of *Esmoreit*.............	117
Appendix II.	Summaries of Romances........................	120
Appendix III.	Chaucer, Gower, and Trivet..................	132
Index	....	135

CHAUCER'S CONSTANCE
AND
ACCUSED QUEENS

CHAPTER I
INTRODUCTORY

THE heroines of medieval fiction are not extremely varied in character. A few well-defined types recur again and again: the amusing, unadmirable matrons of the *fabliaux;* the well-bred, introspective court ladies of Chrétien de Troyes; the strong-minded Saracen princesses who abjure fatherland and religion to marry Christian knights; the young maidens who are rescued from imminent danger abroad or awarded as prizes in tournaments at home. Among other equally popular types is the widely celebrated, attractive figure of an innocent, persecuted queen, whose character and story arouse pity rather than mirth or excitement merely. Heroines of this type appear in narratives which center about the steadfastness of sorely tried virtue. They are usually the wives or mothers of heroes, and the tale of their undeserved suffering at the hands of a persecutor or a credulous and suspicious husband, frequently evoked the best efforts and warmest sympathy of medieval poets. Moreover, the great number of tales about queens who are falsely accused by a villain, condemned by a husband to death or exile, and rescued by a son or champion, indicates the literary popularity of these situations.

Of all heroines in medieval literature who are falsely accused and triumphantly vindicated, none is more famous than Chaucer's Constance, whose loneliness and dignity under persecution have aroused sympathy in generations of readers, and whose white face, as she confronted accusation in exile, inspired one of the finest passages in the *Canterbury Tales:*[1]

> Have ye nat seyn som-tyme a pale face,
> Among a press, of him that hath be lad
> Toward his death, wher-as him gat no grace,
> And swich a colour in his face hath had
> Men mighte knowe his face that was bistad
> Amonges alle the faces in that route?
> So stant Custance, and loketh hir aboute.

[1] *Man of Law's Tale*, ll. 547 ff.

The story of her sufferings and exile, which the Man of Law told to his fellow pilgrims, is well known to all students of English literature. We can imagine these men and women (even the most incorrigible of them, like the Miller and the Reeve) following the tale with respectful sympathy; yet, in spite of the warmth and feeling that pervade the story, some episodes must have appeared incredible, even to the most absorbed listener. Even less credible, of course, do they appear to us. Let us remind ourselves of the plot of the Man of Law's tale as a story of an accused queen:

Some Saracen merchants who have been trading in Rome tell their Sultan of the beauty and goodness of Constance, the Emperor's daughter. The Sultan thereupon determines to marry her, even if he must adopt Christianity to win her. The marriage is arranged, and Constance leaves Rome for the Orient, since the good of Christendom requires this sacrifice of her. But the Sultan's mother, angry at her son's plan, changes the wedding feast into a bloody ambush from which only Constance escapes alive. She is placed in a rudderless boat and cast adrift on the sea. After more than three years she lands on the shore of England. Here the Constable of Northumberland and his wife Hermengild shelter her. She converts them to Christianity; Hermengild works a miracle soon after her conversion by restoring sight to a blind man.

Constance is courted by a member of the Constable's household who, being rebuffed, takes revenge in a horrible fashion. He cuts Hermengild's throat while she is asleep, and lays the bloody knife beside Constance. He accuses her of the deed; but a hand miraculously smites him dead after his false oath. This divine interposition causes King Alla to declare Constance innocent, and to be converted himself.

King Alla marries Constance, but his mother Donegild resents the marriage bitterly. While the King is away at war, Constance bears a son. The messenger who carries the tidings to Alla stays over night at the castle of Donegild, who changes his letters while he lies in a drunken sleep so that they report the birth of a monster. On the messenger's return, she changes her son's letters to an order for the exiling of Constance once more in her rudderless boat. She departs with her young son. During her voyage, she is molested by a renegade thief who boards her ship to demand her love; but, in his struggles with her, he falls into the sea and is drowned. Constance arrives in Rome, and is harbored in the house of a friendly senator. When her husband comes to Rome as penitent, having executed his mother for her treason, he finds his wife and son there, and the family is reunited.

Of the many improbable episodes in this plot, perhaps none is more improbable than the accusation of Donegild, written in the messenger's exchanged letter. That Constance is supposed to have borne a monster, on the accusation of a jealous old mother-in-law, is a trait suggesting the plot of a primitive folk-tale rather than a literary romance of such high artistic merit as Chaucer's. The presence of this trait in the *Man of Law's Tale* and in many of its analogues in the Middle Ages, suggests the presence of a problem in folk-lore in the midst of literary problems.

The *Man of Law's Tale* and its analogues have been the subject of much scholarly research in the past seventy-five years. Tyrwhitt did not know of Chaucer's source; but in 1845 Bäckström pointed it out in his notes to the Swedish folk-book [2] *Helena Antonia af Constantinopel*.[3] There he discussed the *Life of Constance* by Nicholas Trivet, and arrived at the conclusion that the story was of English, or rather of Anglo-Saxon, origin. The publication of Trivet's work by the Chaucer Society in 1872 opened the way for a comparison of Chaucer with his Anglo-French source and with the similar story told in a Latin *Life of Offa I*.[4] A very suggestive inquiry was made by de Puymaigre,[5] who assembled a body of folk-tales resembling, in general outlines, the Constance-romance, but more particularly the large group of versions outside of Chaucer and Trivet, in which the heroine runs away from her father in the beginning because he wants to marry her. It became apparent that the problem of Chaucer's Constance is closely connected with that of many other heroines in romances with this startling beginning. The Constance-legend must therefore be understood to include all parallels to Chaucer's tale, whether, as in most cases, the opening action uses the Incestuous Father or (as in Chaucer) the Wicked Mother-in-law as first persecutor.

The first extended inquiry into the medieval cycle of romances which begin with an Incestuous Father and include exile and accusation of the heroine by an exchanged letter, was made by Suchier,[6]

---

[2] The term *folk-book* is used throughout to designate the popular prose redactions of romances which appeared in print from the fifteenth century on.
[3] *Svenska Folkböcker*, Stockholm, 1845, I, 221 ff.

[4] Published at the same time by the Chaucer Society.
[5] *La Fille aux Mains Coupées, Revue de l'Histoire des Religions*, X, 1884, 193-208.
[6] Preface to *La Manekine* of Beaumanoir, Soc. des An. Textes Fr.

who analyzed the type-plot and compared it with similar folk-tales. This study was followed in 1902 by Gough's *On the Constance-Saga*,[7] which, largely dependent on Suchier's matter and method, traced the romance back to an hypothetical Anglian folk-tale in England before the Conquest. In 1906, Edith Rickert approached the cycle from another point of view in her edition of the related Middle English romance *Emare*, for which she suggested additional analogues and sources. In the meantime, other versions of the story had been published and republished; and students became acquainted with other heroines who fled from their fathers, married foreign princes, were falsely accused, and went into a second exile with their children. Scholars began to compare the general Constance-cycle with other families of romances about persecuted wives. Siefken,[8] for instance, studied the types of persecuted ladies to be found in Middle English fiction; but his work arrives at no definite conclusion, and it suffers from its limitation to English romance. More helpful is Stefanović's study[9] of the kindred Florence de Rome type of romance and his contribution of new and significant Slavic märchen analogues, which are important also for the Constance-cycle. Since this investigation, no further work, so far as I know, has been done on the sources and analogues of Chaucer's version.[10]

There has hitherto been no attempt to survey all the types of accused and innocent queens in medieval romance, or to investigate the significance of folk-lore traits (such as the accusation of monstrous birth) as survivals. Sandras, an earlier commentator on Chaucer's *Man of Law's Tale*,[11] suggested, it is true, the general relation of Constance to the heroines of *Parise la Duchesse*, *Roman de la Violette*, and *Chevalier au Cygne*. He even hinted that the treason of Donegild in Chaucer is borrowed from Matabrune's in the last cycle,[12] because each is a mother-in-law persecuting her son's wife. The similarity is indeed significant: not because one

---

[7] *Palaestra*, XXXIII, 1902.
[8] *Der Konstanze-Griseldistypus in der engl. Lit. bis auf Shakspere*, Rathenow, 1902; *Das geduldige Weib in der engl. Lit.*, Rathenow, 1903.
[9] *Anglia*, XXXV, 483-525; *Rom. Forschungen*, XXIX, 461-556.

[10] Cf. J. Koch, *Anglia*, XXXVII, 1925, 193 ff.: *Der gegenwärtige Stand der Chaucer-forschung* (a review of contributions to Chaucer-research since 1908).
[11] E. G. Sandras, *Étude sur G. Chaucer considéré comme Imitateur des Trouvères*, Paris, 1859, 203-214.
[12] Sandras, *op. cit.*, 213.

is the source of the other, but because both testify independently to the existence of this märchen formula in romance. The hint of Sandras is valuable because it suggests the need for a systematic study of the accusations brought against all queens in romance, and of the motives of the accusers.

The present work is an attempt to make such a study. It will depend in large part on the research of many who have investigated the material in each of the various subordinate groups of the story. But my aim is different from theirs. It is not my purpose merely to review a certain number of close and obviously similar analogues to Chaucer's *Man of Law's Tale*, or to construct a series of genealogical tables for related literary versions. I shall try rather to point out the similar *themes* of story-telling about accused queens in many types of folk-tales; to find out what light is shed on such themes by the study of primitive custom and belief; and to trace the modifications of these themes in medieval romance. Much of the material used here in the section on romance is of course familiar to students of medieval literature; but some of it is new. A section of the Netherlandish romance *Seghelijn van Jerusalem*,[13] which contains a heroine modeled on Florence de Rome and Parise la Duchesse, is discussed for the first time in this connection; the Latin letter of Jacob Wimfeling about an accused heroine, which has been generally neglected since its publication,[14] is also included in this study; the long unpublished romance of *Theseus de Cologne* contributes three new heroines to place beside Constance; and other accused ladies like Hirlanda of Brittany or Idda of Tockenburg, usually overlooked, or unknown to scholars on this side of the Atlantic, are reintroduced.

The folk-lore of accused queens also requires a more adequate discussion than it has yet received. It is necessary to look for parallels outside of romance for episodes, such as accusations of cannibalism or animal birth, which have hitherto caused natural surprise among modern readers of the romances. Much in these medieval traditions can be found also in folk-tales, imbedded in apparently more primitive material; and these folk-tales must be

[13] Ed. Verdam, Leiden, 1878.
[14] *Zeitschrift für vergleichende Literaturgeschichte*, IV, 1891, 342-355. Stefanović mentions the version (contained in a MS. in the British Museum) in his study of *Florence de Rome*.

studied as well, if one is searching for parallels to the weird customs, fantastic notions, and primitive survivals persistent in courtly medieval fiction. If a high-born dame is accused in a romance or fairy tale of killing her child or eating it, there must be a reason for this astonishing charge; and if the lady thus accused fails to defend herself, there must be a reason for her irrational silence. Only an extended inquiry into all similar folk-tales, and into popular custom and folk-lore, will yield explanations of these things. I realize fully the dangers of this method. Most folk-tales recovered from popular tradition were not written down before the nineteenth century, and are consequently less primitive in time and in their present form than a French romance of the thirteeth century. It is also true that unrelated popular tales from parts of the world so widely sundered as the Malay Islands and South America, cannot be considered as possible ancestors for a masterpiece of Middle English verse in the fourteenth century. But we are nevertheless justified, I believe, in summoning whatever help we can obtain from the study of märchen. A common denominator exists between Chaucer and an African folk-tale, perhaps: the heritage of a similar past of half-forgotten customs, superstitions, and beliefs, which display a remarkable similarity the world over. If one is careful to employ comparison only for the purpose of obtaining a concept of this wider psychological background, shared in its general features by all primitive peoples, one may draw significant inferences from the illustrative use of märchen. And, in the survivals of primitive custom and psychology, European folk-tales are quite as rich as any others. For this reason, late though they are in print, these tales may fairly be considered old enough in substance to be placed before medieval romance, and below it, as a foundation for this discussion.

The present study will therefore endeavor to answer the following questions: "Of what were queens accused in märchen and romances? Who accused them, and why?" The answers to these questions will, I think, throw some light on the genesis and development of a plot such as Chaucer has made familiar to us, and on the reasons for various absurdities of motivation in a story full of realistic characterization and genuine pathos. We shall see that in folk-tales many queens are accused and exiled, like Constance, because of the enmity of a jealous mother-in-law; others because of the vindictiveness of a witch or demon or stepmother, or the breaking of a tabu by the heroine herself. The accusations brought against these ladies are: witchcraft, the bearing of animals instead of children, cannibalism, or child-murder. In romances, we shall find some of these old accusers and accusations—elements more pertinent to the fiction of primitive peoples than of civilized courts and society—and some new ones besides. Accusations of treason and infidelity, which are naturally all but unknown in the more primitive society of folk-tales, often replace those mentioned above; and ambitious traitors and rejected lovers appear as accusers in later types of narrative.

This change can be observed only if we consider all cycles of stories about persecuted queens, with the appropriate märchen background. The study of one cycle alone, such as the frequently analyzed Constance-group, is not sufficiently enlightening. And it happens that the Constance-group, famous though it is, does not present the most advantageous point of departure for a comparison between fairy tales and romance. Chaucer's story is a complex of several motifs—some of them modified—which must be kept apart in this discussion. A simpler plot would serve better for the statement of the problem. Such a plot is to be found in a short piece of medieval dramatic literature, written during Chaucer's lifetime in the Low Countries across the English Channel, which also combines themes from märchen and romance. I refer to the old Flemish play of *Esmoreit*, which briefly celebrates the accusation of a queen and her vindication by her son. Little has been done to explain the source of the plot,[15] although students of the medieval stage have discussed it from time to time for their own purposes.[16]

---

[15] Contained in the Hulthem MS. (early 15th century) of the Bibliothèque Royale, Brussels. Printed in French translation, *Messager des Sciences et des Arts de la Belgique*, Ghent, 1835, 6-40. Editions in the original language: Hoffmann von Fallersleben, *Horae Belgicae*, VI; H. E. Moltzer, *De middelnederlandsche dramatische Poezie*, 1868-1875; P. Leendertz, *Middelnederlandsche dramatische Poezie*, 1899-1900; separate printing by Kaakebeen and Ligthard, 1906, 1918, and 1924.

[16] Leendertz collected a number of analogues from French romance, which may be found in the introduction to his edition. Prietzch (*Neophilologus*, Oct., 1921) argues that the materials for the story came from *Jan uut den Vergiere*, a romance preserved in the form of a Flemish folk-book. Both essays suffer from a neglect of the study of analogues from märchen and romances.

The text has recently been made available in an English translation [17] which preserves much of the charm and flavor of the original. It tells this story:

Esmoreit is the young son of the old King of Sicily, whose nephew Robbrecht had hoped to become King himself if his uncle had died childless. Robbrecht determines, therefore, to destroy the infant heir who interferes with his plans. Meantime, a new danger threatens the child. Far away in the East, a heathen King has been horrified to learn from his court astrologer that this same child is doomed to kill him and marry his daughter. He sends the astrologer to get the child, who is at this moment being threatened with death by Robbrecht. The emissary stays the murderous villain's hand, buys the child from him, and returns to the East. Esmoreit is confided to the care of the King's daughter, Damiet.

When Esmoreit is missed, Robbrecht commits a triple villainy against the Queen. He tells the King, first, that she killed the child herself; second, that she is plotting to kill her husband; third, that she is guilty of infidelity. The King believes his nephew's words, summons the Queen, and sentences her to lasting imprisonment. So Robbrecht is left to dominate the situation as he chooses.

But time brings a solution. When Esmoreit has grown up (for he is allowed to grow up, in spite of the heathen King's fear of him), he falls in love with his foster sister, learns from her that he is, supposedly, a foundling, and departs with his baby clothes to seek his parents. He chances to find his mother's prison. She speaks to him from it, and a recognition scene quickly follows. This, of course, leads to her vindication; and, when Damiet and the astrologer join Esmoreit in Sicily, the full villainy of Robbrecht is revealed. He is properly punished with death; and Esmoreit marries Damiet after both have been converted to Christianity.

Even a brief summary reveals several inconsistencies in the plot. What becomes of the prophecy that Esmoreit will kill his father-in-law? The author forgets it, evidently, or is unable to combine it with other elements of the action. Why, if the heathen King really fears the fulfilment of the prophecy, does he tempt fate by giving Esmoreit into his daughter's hands to be reared? Clearly this is an instance of over-motivation, a duplication of excuses for removing Esmoreit from his heritage and sending him into exile.

[17] *An Ingenious Play of Esmoreit, the King's Son of Sicily*, translated by Harry Morgan Ayres, The Hague, 1924.

But the chief difficulties of the plot concern the villain Robbrecht and the Queen. The heaped-up accusations against Esmoreit's mother are dramatically unnecessary. A villain need not add the charge of a mythical lover, if the King already believes that his wife actually killed her own child. Either of these serious charges would be enough. All of the elements of the drama are to be found in fairy tales except Robbrecht, who seems to be an alien intruder. Scheming, blackhearted villains are not common at the courts of the fairy-tale kings (even when the kings are fantastically cruel); but they are quite at home in the society of a later form of literature—the *chansons de geste*. The persecutor who writes the forged letter in Chaucer's *Man of Law's Tale* is the mother-in-law, a typical märchen character, and her accusation that the young Queen has borne a monster is a typical märchen accusation. The ambitious villain Robbrecht, on the other hand, is an accuser introduced from romance into a folk-tale plot; and one of his accusations, that the Queen has committed adultery, is typical of the romances to which he properly belongs. But Robbrecht utters a second accusation less consonant with the courtly society of medieval romance: the charge of child-murder. This incongruous accusation is, as we shall see, quite common and natural in its proper setting of märchen characters. Child-murder and giving birth to animals are two of the most important accusations occurring in the folk-tales to be examined in the next chapter. Our first task must be to find out what characters make these accusations in folk-tales, and why.[18]

---

[18] For a statement of the answer to this question, see summary of results, pp. 113-114.

CHAPTER II
ACCUSED QUEENS IN FOLK-TALES

A. THE ACCUSATION OF INFANTICIDE

THE answers to our first question, "Why are queens accused and exiled in folk-tales?" are various; but they are all characteristic of primitive conditions. One of these we have already heard from Robbrecht's lips: the accusation of child-murder. Here is another instance:[1]

A stepmother witch curses three brothers so that they are under a spell to spend most of each day fighting. They wander away from home. Their little sister follows them, determined to help them. At last she finds them. They tell her to leave them, for fear that they may hurt her unintentionally when their pugilistic fury comes on them; but they tell her that she can unspell them if she keeps silence, under all trials and temptations, for nine years.

A king's son marries her. His stepmother, who is hostile to the young Queen, cuts off her first child's foot, smears her with the blood, and thrusts the foot into her mouth. Then she accuses her of killing and eating the child. The young Queen can say nothing. The same thing happens a second time; but still the King is unwilling to have her killed. He finally yields to his stepmother's urgency. As his consort is about to be hanged, the nine years are at last complete. Her brothers come to her, freed from the witch's power; angels appear to vindicate her, and carry all the good people to heaven; but the evil stepmother is cast into hell.

Another story from the same part of the world:[2]

A girl has been pledged to a witch by her father before birth (in return for help). At the age of fifteen, she is claimed by the witch. In the house of her mistress, she opens a forbidden door and sees a corpse which lifts its head and says oracularly, "Don't confess!" When the witch asks her whether she has opened the door she accordingly replies "No!" She is driven out into the forest, naked and dumb.

A king's son finds her. He takes her home and marries her. Each time she bears a child the witch appears and says, "Do you confess?" The

---

[1] August von Löwis of Menar, *Finnische und Estnische Volksmärchen*, Jena, 1922, 259. An Esthonian tale.
[2] *Ibid.*, 100. A Finnish tale.

girl always replies "No!" Then the child is taken away and bones are left beside the mother, as if she had eaten her child. Her royal husband endures this until the third occurrence, in spite of court gossip. Then he orders his wife to be burnt. As the fire is being lit, the witch appears again with her laconic question. The condemned Queen gives her still more laconic answer. Vanquished by so much fortitude, the witch restores both the children and the power of speech to the Queen, and puts out the fire.

From Greece comes this tale:[3]

A Prince riding in the forest finds an apparently dead maiden lying in a coffin. (She has been bewitched by the jealous mythical "mother of Erotas," who envied her beauty and gave her a golden ring to induce this profound trance.) By chance, the Prince removes her ring and she comes to life. He marries her, and is so devoted to her that he neglects his mother. In revenge, she goes into the young Queen's room and cuts off the heads of her young children and throws them on their mother's bed. The next morning, the King sees this, hears his mother's accusations, and believes all too easily. The hands of his wife are cut off and sewed into a sack, together with her children's corpses. She is driven forth, still preserving her irrational silence (for there is no spell here to tie her tongue). A monk whom she meets restores her hands to her mutilated arms, and her children to life. With his magic staff, he creates a castle for her and disappears. Here her royal husband finds her one day as he chances to pass by. She breaks her silence at last and tells her tale. He has his mother put into a barrel of pitch and thrown into the sea.

We shall meet this handless heroine again, both in fairy tales and in courtly romance related to Chaucer's *Man of Law's Tale*. She is the victim of many persecutions and many accusations. For the present, it is necessary to notice merely that she is definitely connected with the barbaric accusation of child-murder. A more typical heroine, who does not lose her hands, appears in this Arabian tale:[4]

A Princess has put herself into the power of a persecuting dragon. On her bridal eve, the dragon appears and starts to carry her away. She flees into a neighboring room, and calls on a fairy for aid. The fairy instructs her how to kill the dragon, on condition that her firstborn child be sur-

---

[3] Bernhard Schmidt, *Griechische Märchen, Sagen und Volkslieder*, Leipzig, 1877, 110.

[4] *Arabische Märchen*, M. Gladbach, 1920, 49. (Collected and translated by Hella Mors.)

rendered. The need is great and the young Queen yields. When the child disappears, the King's hostile mother immediately accuses her of murdering it, and reduces her to the position of slave in the kitchen. The heroine's patience under her great trial softens the heart of the fairy. The child is restored to its mother, who is thereupon reinstated beside the King.

In this tale from Africa, the accusation seems more consonant with characters and background:[5]

A widow has taken to cowherding to support herself, and she hopes to marry the owner of the cows. So she tries to ruin the man's wife. When the latter bears twins, the ambitious widow puts them in a box and sets them afloat on the river. She also smears blood over the face and hands of the wife and accuses her of eating them. The wife is exiled and reduced to ass-tending; the ambitious widow marries the cattle-owner.

The drifting children are found by the riverside, and grow up to be mighty warriors. They are sent ahead as spies into their father's land. They find their exiled mother, hear her tale, get help from her in the attack, and take her away with them.

The prominence of the exposed children in this last tale gives it particular interest. The child who is exposed or otherwise shares in the misfortune of his mother often grows up to be her savior and vindicator.

Feminine jealousy is often the cause of barbarous accusations in Mohammedan countries. A less favored wife steals the children from the favorite, and brings the charge of child-murder to ruin her rival.[6] But this variant of the type is naturally not to be found in monogamous Europe. Even when such traditions in Europe are patently derived from the East, they are modified to fit European institutions. So it happens that the popular ramifications of a single Oriental tale are often very enlightening for the study of European folk-lore, since the motives substituted to avoid the postulate of a polygamous society are in themselves strictly popular and European, quite varied, and often extremely primitive.

[5] Carl Meinhof, *Africanische Märchen*, Jena, 1921, no. 80. The same story appears in A. C. Hollis's *The Masai*, Oxford, 1905, 177. The jealous woman is, however, a co-wife with her rival from the beginning of the story.
[6] Cf. J. Rivière, *Recueil de Contes Populaires de la Kabylie du Djurdjura*, Paris, 1882, 71.

What now of the state of society in which stories such as these must have originated? One may fairly suppose that, in such a level of culture, both the accusation and the deed itself might occur as a harsh reality. It would not always be merely the fantastic invention of a witch or villain-accuser. Usually, when such a bit of plot-mechanism is found repeated often enough in not-too-similar, not-too-proximate tales, one begins to suspect that it is a survival: the trace of a custom senescent or abandoned, perhaps, but not forgotten. And it is remarkable how long such cruel customs, with their irrational logic of life and death and causation, survive in the traditions of more enlightened times. They undergo softening or modification, it is true; but their original form is clearly visible. The Queen is no longer actually guilty of killing or eating her children, but she is at least accused of the crime as if it were credible and probable and not too astonishing for the world in which she lives. A King no longer fears and persecutes his son as a matter of course, seeing in the boy a reincarnation of himself which threatens his own identity; but he listens to the witch or astrologer who prophesies his death at the boy's hands, and he acts on the prophecy with all the vigor of one who hears in it the behest of an ancient, logical, accepted custom. Prophecies and false accusations and warnings are often the voice of a dying custom, once universal and still potent as the dynamic force to motivate a tale. With this in mind, we may discover a reason for the absurd suspicion cast upon our suffering queens.

That suspicion savors more of cannibalism than of courtly romance. Infanticide is not a pleasant subject to discuss, but the testimony of folk-tales must not be overlooked, since evidence is to be found there as well as in scientific reports of investigators among savage tribes. Various reasons are given in story and fact for this repellent practice. In European tradition, traces of such customs still survive:

1. *Lit. Orale de la Picardie* (Henry Carnoy, Paris, 1883) p. 229. A boy is killed and cooked by his mother in punishment for childish idleness and deception.

Ibid., p. 236. A variation of the same theme. A whistle made of the murdered child's bones tells his sad fate when anyone blows it.

2. *Russische Volksmärchen* (A. von Löwis of Menar, Jena, 1921)

no. 3. During a famine, a mother and father kill their son and eat him. They spare their daughter, because they really care for her. She buries her brother's bones and waters them. From the grave a dove flies out and sings an accusing song far and wide until the neighbors come and put the parents to death.

3. *Lit. Orale de la Haute Bretagne* (P. Sébillot, Paris, 1881) p. 223. A boy is killed and cooked by his mother for a bit of childish deception in the matter of faggot-gathering, and his sister piously collects his bones.

4. *Griechische und albanische Märchen* (J. G. von Hahn, Leipzig, 1864) no. 1. A father has a sudden desire for human flesh. He pursues his son and daughter, who escape with the help of their dog.[7]

5. *Kaukasische Märchen* (A. Dirr, Jena, 1920) no. 16. A man and his wife have two children, a son and a daughter. One day the wife says, "I am sick. I want flesh."—"What flesh?"—"My son's flesh." The man kills his son and serves him to his wife as food. The little girl finds the finger of her brother, recognizes it, wraps it up, and takes it to the churchyard. There it turns into a bird that sings sweetly. It earns a bundle of needles by singing to the needle maker, and blinds its parents by blowing needles into their eyes.

6. *Lit. Orale de la Picardie*, p. 252. A man and his wife are too poor to support their children. They decide to lose them in the forest, so that they may be relieved of the need of filling so many hungry mouths. The first time, the abandoned youngsters find their way home again; the second time, they are more effectually shaken off by the parents, and wander into a world of adventures here irrelevant.—This opening situation is common in fairy tales; instances might be multiplied indefinitely.

It becomes plain from these tales still current among the folk of civilized nations, that there must be some reason for the seemingly incredible accusation of child-murder. This accusation can be explained, I think, by primitive customs. The parallels between fairy tales and fact are too interesting and significant to be overlooked. Whatever the cause may be, infanticide is certainly a widespread practice among contemporary savage peoples. We read in a discussion of Nigerian native life [8] that the parents of four small daughters are accused of eating them when the children disappear in succession; and more important still, the whole village believes that the crime was actually committed. In such cases, the sober

---

[7] Cf. von Hahn's collection, nos. 32 and 36; Klara Stroebe, *Nordische Märchen*, Jena, 1919, II, no. 48; P. Zaunert, *Deutsche Märchen seit Grimm*, Jena, 1919, 250.

[8] A. J. M. Tremearne, *Hansa Superstitions and Customs*, London, 1913.

assumption of the *possibility* of the crime is as important as its existence in fact. Otherwise the rôle of the credulous king in the folk-tales remains incomprehensible. Such anecdotes recall the teknophagous parents in Balkan märchen. Many other verified examples of the same sort may be found in that storehouse of primitive human material, Sir J. G. Frazer's *The Golden Bough*.[9] The following illustrations will indicate clearly enough the universality of the practice of infanticide and some of the motives which lead to it. The customs indicate that child-murder was once a respectable act, not always a subject for accusation.

In some tribes of New South Wales, the eating of the firstborn child of every woman was formerly a tribal religious ceremony. (R. Brough Smyth, *Aborigines of Victoria*, II, 311.)

Among the natives of the districts around the Paroo and Warrego Rivers, also in New South Wales, the firstborn child of a young wife was formerly strangled. (E. Curr, *The Australian Race*, II, 182. *Ibid*., II, 119.)

In India, down to the nineteenth century, the custom of sacrificing a firstborn child to the Ganges was common. (*Folklore*, XIII, 63; also W. Crooke, *Popular Religion and Folklore of Northern India*, II, 169.)

In a Chinese state called Khai-muh, east of Yush, it was once customary to devour firstborn sons. And west of Kiao-Chi "There was a realm of man-eaters, where the firstborn son was, as a rule, chopped to pieces and eaten, and his younger brothers were nevertheless regarded to have fulfilled their fraternal duties towards him." (J. J. M. de Groot, *Religious System of China*, II, 679; IV, 364 and 365.)

The Borans, on the southern borders of Abyssinia, propitiate a sky-spirit called Wak by sacrificing their children and cattle to him. When a man of any standing marries, he is expected to expose the children who are born in the first few years, to die in the bush. (*Geog. Journal*, XXIII, 1904, 567 ff.)

The Kerre, Bana, and Bashada, three tribes in southern Abyssinia, strangle their firstborn children. The Kerre cast the bodies into the river Omo, where they are eaten by crocodiles; but the intention does not seem to be a sacrifice to the crocodiles. The other two tribes expose their children in the forest. (C. H. Stigand, *To Abyssinia through an Unknown Land*, London, 1910, p. 243.)

The natives of Rook, an island off the coast of New Guinea, buried their firstborn children whom they killed instead of eating them. They killed every alternate child thereafter. (*Annales de la Propagation de la Foi*, XXVII, 1855, 368 ff.)

[9] Third edition, 1920, IV, 179-191.

In Queensland, among the aboriginal tribes, a woman's first child was nearly always exposed to die. (A. W. Howitt, *Native Tribes of South East Australia*, p. 750.)

In Polynesia the custom of infanticide did, and still does, prevail widely. Frazer suggests that the custom of abdicating the rights of chieftainship in favor of a newborn son may have led to the practice. If that is the reason, we have here an instance of the fear-motive that becomes so strikingly evident in the stories of exposed children who grow up in spite of their parents: in the Oedipus-myth, for instance. Whatever the reason, the early missionaries estimated that two-thirds of the children born were killed by their parents. W. Ellis (in his *Polynesian Researches*, London, 1832) tells of three women who, together, had put to death twenty-one children.

Some tribes killed children simply to avoid the trouble of rearing them, especially if the mother were burdened with more than one very small infant at a time. "It is infanticide which is resorted to for the purpose of keeping down the number of a family. And here we may say that the number is kept down, not with any idea at all of regulating the food supply, so far as the adults are concerned, but simply from the point of view that, if the mother is suckling one child, she cannot properly provide food for another, quite apart from the question of carrying two children about." (Spencer and Gillen, *Native Tribes of Central Australia*, p. 264.) It is well to remember that savages are not gifted with economic forethought or understanding of the relation of population to food supply. Although Polynesians are said to have practised infanticide because of the restricted space for a growing population,[10] most primitive people show a consciousness of this relation only when they are already hard-pressed by famine. Then, as in the familiar fairy tales, the children are simply eaten. "In the Wotjobaluk tribe, infants were killed in the old time, no difference being made between boys and girls. If a couple had a child, either boy or girl, say ten years old, and a baby was born to them, it might be killed and cooked for the elder brother or sister to eat." (A. W. Howitt, *Native Tribes of South-east Australia*, p. 749.)

When girls and boys were not treated alike in the important matter of being killed or allowed to live, the reason is often to be found in the prejudice against girls as useless non-combatants. On the other hand, girls were often spared more readily because they would later bring a good marriage price. (R. H. Corington, *The Melanesians*, Oxford, 1891, p. 229.)

But this reason for sparing them is admittedly an indication of comparative advancement. "The long-headed, cold-hearted calculation, which

---

[10] See also E. J. Eyre, *Journals of Expeditions of Discovery into Central Australia*, London, 1845, II, 324; Frazer's *Totemism and Exogamy*, London, 1910, IV, 77.

ACCUSED QUEENS IN FOLK-TALES 19

spares boys because in years to come they will grow up to fight and hunt, or girls because they will fetch a round price in the marriage market, belongs to a higher stage of intellectual, if not moral evolution than the rude savagery to which the origin of exogamy must be referred." [11] No Australian tribe was ever known to store up food for a time of dearth; so infanticide was hardly practised on the principles of Malthus.

The most common causes of infanticide were: a desire to avoid the care of rearing the children; fear that they might be ancestors reincarnated or might anticipate succession to the chieftainship; prejudice against girls because they would not become warriors; a pressing famine; and, very commonly, a desire to sacrifice to gods or to spirits of water or forest. The exposure of children in rivers or jungles reminds one of children set afloat or wilfully lost by too-poor parents in folk-tales. Only, the motive discovered by a glance at tribal customs (sacrifice) seems more genuine and ancient than lack of food. Certainly a provident restriction of population was no motive [12] among the tribes just discussed. Fear seems to be one reason for child-sacrifice: fear of the gods among even such civilized people as the Carthaginians; fear of one's child as potential rival and successor, especially among people who believed strongly in transmigration of the soul. "At Whydah, on the slave coast of West Africa, where the doctrine of reincarnation is firmly held, it has happened that a child has been put to death because the fetish doctors declared it to be the king's father come to life again. The king naturally could not submit to be pushed from the throne by his predecessor in this fashion; so he compelled his supposed parent to return to the realm of the dead." [13]

No one would be so rash as to assume a direct connection between the customs of the Slave Coast of Africa, and folk-tales current among the evolved races of Europe. Parents in European märchen do not eat or expose their children on land and water because African black men put *their* offspring to strange and seemingly inhuman uses. But European tradition shows the survival of similar customs, in tales told to frighten unruly children. Human sacrifice to rivers can be clearly perceived in the surviving legends

[11] *Ibid.,* IV, 82.
[12] *The Golden Bough,* IV, 188.
[13] *Missions Catholiques,* XVI, 1884, 259.

of the Germans. The Nickert or Nickelmann is supposed to have a great passion for pulling down unwary children into the green depths as his prey, a sacrifice which he seizes if it is not willingly given.[14] "Kinder dürfen nicht zu nah ans Wasser gehen, denn da unten sitzt der schwartze Nickelmann, der schnappt nach ihnen," [15] we are told; and it is not impossible to feel the thrill of terror and curiosity with which a youngster might receive this warning from parents who are unconsciously echoing an ancestral age of child-sacrifice. In ancient times, the story goes, people sacrificed a black chicken yearly: but once they forgot, and the Nickelmann claimed a human substitute in the shape of an unfortunate creature who was drowned in the waters.[16] A grim reality existed once to make possible the exquisite opening lyric of Schiller's *Wilhelm Tell*.

To sum up: in a certain body of folk-tales, a queen is falsely accused of killing, or killing and eating, her own children. As the instances quoted would indicate, the king's jealous mother is usually the malignant accuser. In other tales, the heroine is persecuted by a witch or a dragon or a stepmother or a rival or a rival wife; but never, as far as I know, by a scheming courtier. Side by side with the stories in which the mother did not commit the crime of infanticide, there are tales in which the crime is actually committed, or at least contemplated. These tales serve to make more vivid and comprehensible the first group, in which the false and monstrous accusation is so readily believed. In them, the reasons are not always given; but among the motives suggested are famine, punishment for the child, and fear of the child (a father's fear that the child will cause his ruin). These motives can be traced still among primitive folk: famine, fear, a simple desire to be rid of the child, and an obligation to placate spirits of earth and water (forests and rivers) by human sacrifice. This last motive is not distinctly expressed in folk-tales, to be sure; but we may be reasonably certain that the widespread superstitions about water spirits and child victims are descended from forgotten customs of the sort. And the promising of children to the devil or to some other malevolent power before birth (as in the second

---

[14] Kühn und Schwartz, *Norddeutsche Sagen*, Leipzig, 1848, 92, 94, 174.
[15] *Ibid.*, 172.
[16] Cf. *The Golden Bough*, IV, 38; J. W. Wolf, *Niederländische Sagen*, Leipzig, 1843, 14; R. Wilhelm, *Chinesische Volksmärchen*, no. 52—a clear example of custom living on in tradition.

Finnish story quoted) is another form assumed by child-sacrifice in popular tradition.

In a certain sense, the investigation thus far has yielded only negative results. We have found many parallels to the accusation of child-murder brought by Robbrecht: illuminating parallels; constant reminders that a very thin line separates primitive legends and beliefs from the more civilized literature of Western Europe in the Middle Ages. But we have found no companion-figure for Robbrecht himself, the traitor from whose mouth issues the astonishingly primitive and incongruous accusation of infanticide. The very absence of this figure in the fairy tales has a real significance.

B. The Accusation of Animal Birth

A second accusation brought against unhappy, nameless queens in fairy tales is even more fantastic than the first, to our present way of thinking, although it is to be found in Chaucer. It is the accusation, namely, that the unfortunate lady has brought into the world monsters or animals instead of children. The charge occurs in many tales from all parts of the world, and is nearly always believed by the royal husband. Here, for instance, is a Turkish tale, in which the motive is feminine jealousy:[17]

A man has no children. So he buys a second wife, who naturally evokes the envy of the first. When the new favorite bears twins, the envious one substitutes a dead snake, boxes up the children, and has them thrown into the sea. They are found on the shore by another childless man whose wife's dream had sent him looking there. The man adopts the children. Their real mother is disgraced by the supposed unnatural birth, and driven into exile. Shepherds take care of her.

One day the companions of the boy taunt him as a foundling. He is impatient to find his own family. So he and his sister go on their journey guided by a dream, and the son finds his mother, besides dragons to encounter, and riches, and a wife.

In a Berber story, the boy reinstates his mother as well.[18]

A man has two wives, one of whom bears a son. The father com-

---

[17] I. Kúnos, *Türkische Volksmärchen aus Stambul*, 339.

[18] J. Rivière, *Recueil de Contes Populaires de la Kabylie du Djurdjura*, 39.

mands her to devote herself to the care of the infant while the other wife does the work. This makes the childless wife jealous. She sends the favored one to get water while the husband is away. She takes the child from its cradle and exchanges it with a passing merchant for a half-dead crow. When the husband and the mother come in, they see the bird in the cradle. The other wife says, "Look! She is the mother of a crow!" The crow is killed, and the mother is reduced to a mean place in the household.

Years later the boy learns from his foster-mother, the merchant's wife, that he is not her son. He demands to be taken back to the house where he was so cheaply sold. When food is brought to him there, he says, "I shall not eat unless the other wife is brought in." They protest that she is a bad woman because her child was really a crow, and had assumed its proper shape very soon. "Did the child have a birth mark?" asks the boy; and triumphantly displays his own to prove his identity. Thus he restores his mother to her rightful place.

Such stories are particularly interesting because they reach a solution—the restoration of the wronged lady—through the child himself. This conclusion occurs frequently in both märchen and romance. In Zulu tradition,[19] a chief's wife once gave birth to a huge snake which was cast into a pool and avoided in horror by the people. The mother was disgraced, and had to live in an isolated hut near the gateway of the new village. One day ten children come out of the deserted snake. They seek out their father's village. In some hidden way, they know about their mother's fate, and are able to answer their father's questions and to point her out. The oldest says reproachfully, "I see that my mother was troubled." The father apologizes—and hastily abdicates.

The credulity of the husband in a tale such as this becomes more understandable when one recalls the numberless cases of human mothers in folk-tales who actually do bear animals. In the most primitive type of literature, the possibility is always gravely conceded. A Malay story [20] has a heroine who bears a dog as son; and it is noteworthy that a dog is actually the father as well. Another story in the same collection [21] tells of an ape born of a human mother, who is unspelled and given human shape by mar-

[19] Henry Callaway, *Nursery Tales . . . of the Zulus*, 268.
[20] Paul Hambruch, *Malaiische Märchen aus Madagaskar und Insulinde*, Jena, 1922, no. 60.
[21] *Ibid.*, no. 26.

riage with the king's daughter. The Zulus tell of a snake born of a chief's favorite wife, after three preceding children have been destroyed by a jealous sister, who is a rival wife. The snake-child is unspelled by a girl who is brave enough to marry him: whereupon it appears that the transformation of shape was a device of his mother's to save him from the jealous rival.[22] In Europe, also, there are countless tales which begin with the birth of an animal from a human mother, as the result of an incautiously expressed wish: "I wish I might have a child, even if it were only a cat," or snake, or puppy, or what not. To this family of tales belongs the King Lindorm type, in which the liberation of the animal is brought about by a girl who marries and unspells him.[23] Stories of this type render quite understandable the plausibility which earlier story-tellers, and later ones as well, found in the accusation of an animal birth.

As for the stories in which the charge is brought falsely and malevolently, for one cause or another, they too are multifarious but very similar to one another. One large group, which may be called "The Exchanged Letter," presents a definite plot with a definite logic of sequent events, roughly the same in all instances. When this is true of a popular tale with a rather complex plot, one may suspect a genealogical family relation among the obtainable instances of the type, especially when these instances are not separated by insuperable geographical barriers. And the family relationship among numerous contemporary tales implies descent from a common ancestor, when a fairly complicated plot has maintained its form as persistently the same in outline, even if it is scattered and multiplied in many variant versions.

Let us assume with Bolte and Polívka,[24] for instance, that the ramified variants of the Exchanged Letter story (similar to Chaucer's Constance-story) go back to a single source and locality which are unknown to us. Does that mean necessarily that the group has no significance for an attempt like this, to discover universal thought-ways of primitive story-tellers, through similar beliefs

---

[22] Henry Callaway, *op. cit.*, 321.

[23] E.g., Klara Stroebe, *Nordische Volksmärchen*, no. 1.

[24] Johannes Bolte and Georg Polívka, *Ammerkungen zu den Kinder- und Hausmärchen der Brüder Grimm*, Leipzig, 1913, II, 380.

similarly manifest the world over in stories of independent origin? Must the stories considered be limited to those simpler ones which quite clearly do not stand in any definite genealogical series—which seem to have arisen independently out of similar customs and beliefs? I think not, for two reasons. In the first place, even the "Urmärchen" of the more complicated type is made up of constituent parts which may be closely paralleled in simple independent stories or customs the world over; which are none the less primitive for being used elsewhere as part of a mosaic of such formulae. Thus, the motive used at the beginning of the Exchanged Letter tale in many of its versions (the desire of a king to marry his own daughter) may be found in the classical fables of Hyginus and in the Cinderella-märchen. In the latter case, the heroine escapes from her father with magnificent clothes which serve to dazzle a prince at three successive balls, while she serves by day as kitchen maid in the royal palace. This is but one instance of the ubiquitousness of such formulae. Even if one gifted story-teller at one definite time was responsible for the weaving of such inherited themes into a more elaborate fabric, the strands themselves may be recognized separately and identified elsewhere.

The second reason for attaching some importance to related family groups of stories is this: after the "Urmärchen," in its hypothetical original form, had become current among the various nations of Europe, it was modified here and there, and substitutions were made, and new formulae of equally ancient date were introduced in place of old ones. Thus, at the beginning of the story, the cruel persecuting father or the malevolent stepmother might be substituted for the incestuous father. In this way, the shifting, kaleidoscopic plot becomes anew the repository of varying yet similar motives of independent origin in popular custom. This increases its significance for the student.

The heroine who suffers exile because of an accusation that she has borne animals is commonly the victim of forgery like Donegild's in Chaucer.[25] We may take an Italian tale as a point of departure.[26]

[25] For a bibliography of this type of folk-tale, see Bolte and Polívka, I, 302-311. Only typical variants will be summarized here.

[26] A. de Gubernatis, *Tradizioni Popolari de S. Stefano di Calcinaia*, Rome, 1894, 146.

A King, departing for war, leaves his wife in the care of his mother, who is hostile to the young Queen. The wife bears a son and a daughter. The enraged mother-in-law writes a letter to her son about the event; but, instead of reporting the truth, she says that the Queen has borne puppies. The King is very sad when he receives this piece of news; but, thinking it is his blood as well as hers [he is not primitive enough to suspect animal parenthood for the children, as do some], he replies with a command to have his wife well cared for. Instead, the mother-in-law has her set adrift in a chest with the two children. A fisherman finds them on an island, and cares for them for six years. One day the King comes, and sees his children. He finds his wife and hears the tale of her wrongs; and the family is happily reunited. But the wicked mother-in-law is put to death.

In a second tale from the same country,[27] the King's mother hates her daughter-in-law because she is of peasant birth. Here the old woman herself stirs up the war which calls her son away; and instead of accusing the young mother by letter merely, she actually substitutes dogs for the children, and exposes the babies in the forest. Both of these tales represent a simple and reduced form of the plot. There is, so far, no introduction explaining how the King came to marry the heroine; and the mother-in-law writes an original letter instead of forging an exchanged one. In a Turkish story, we find a more complicated machinery:[28]

To escape marriage with a Dev (demonic creature), a girl flees on a magic horse. She is married by the Padishah of the strange land to which the horse takes her. While her husband is away at war, she bears a son and a daughter. A Tartar messenger is despatched with the good news, but he tarries overnight with the Dev. While the Tartar is asleep, the girl's inhuman lover changes the message to read "two dogs" instead of two children. On the way back, the Tartar spends a second night with the Dev, and the humane commands of the Padishah to have his wife cared for are changed into the curt order: "Cast her and her offspring into the mountains!" The heroine is rescued once more from the Dev by her magic horse. It rides itself to death to serve her, and then changes itself into a palace in which she lives with her two children. When her husband returns home, he learns the truth after a few astonished inquiries and a glance at the changed letter. He sets out to

---

[27] Stanislao Prato, *Quattro Novelline Popolari Livornesi*, Spoleto, 1880, 92-136 (with bibliography). Also Hermann Knust, *Italienische Märchen*, no. 1.

[28] Ignaz Kúnos, *Türkische Volksmärchen aus Stambul*, 172.

find his wife, and finally reaches the magic palace. While he is being served, his wife sends the two children out to ask for food for their wooden horse. "Can these toys eat?" ask the guests. "Can a woman bear dogs?" the children reply; and a recognition scene takes place on the spot.

The changing of the letter during the messenger's sleep is a usual feature of these stories. In this respect, the plot bears a slight resemblance to legends such as the *Dit de l'Empereur Constant*, where a young man is saved from death by a piece of kindly forgery while he is asleep. The Turkish variant has used a demon persecutor in place of the malevolent mother-in-law, just as witch or devil was used in her place as the accuser in the infanticide stories. Further variations may be found in Siberian folk literature. In one tale,[29] the treason and false accusation of animal birth are the work of forty co-wives, helped by a witch-woman. The mother and child are exposed, although the letter had been changed to a command for death. No reason is given for the more humane sentence. It ought logically to proceed from a friend of the heroine—like the Constable in the *Man of Law's Tale*. A second Siberian legend[30] also multiplies the number of persecutors. The girl becomes the victim of a wolf-woman (mother of a wolf she had refused to marry) and of her own mother-in-law. A third variant[31] in the same collection contains the accusation, made by a witch-woman, that the monstrous child is the son of a seven-headed Jelbägän (whatever variety of horror that may be); but the father-in-law who sends the messages is entirely innocent of the charges in them. A blurred tradition from Silesia[32] tells how a King marries the daughter of a poor forest dweller, "although she has no fingers." (The reason for this mutilation is not given; elsewhere we meet a similar disfigurement of the heroine explained in many ways.) His mother is horrified, and

[29] W. Radloff, *Proben der Volksliteratur der türkischen Stämme Südsibiriens*, St. Petersburg, 1866-1870, III, 733. In an Arabic tale translated by Däumling (*Studie über den Typus des "Mädchens ohne Hände,"* Munich, 1912, 57 ff.), the forgery is the work of jealous concubines who write to the kindly, affectionate mother-in-law.
[30] W. Radloff, *Proben der Volksliteratur der türkischen Stämme Südsibiriens*, St. Petersburg, 1866-1870, III, 372.
[31] *Ibid.*, II, 563.
[32] Anton Peter, *Volkstümliches aus Oesterreich-schlesien*, Troppau, 1867, 197.

his neighbors indignantly declare war on him. While the King is away fighting them, the mother orders the young Queen to be taken out into the forest and killed, but she does not avail herself of the use of the forged letter. The murderers spare their victim, of course, and her husband finds her years later, takes her home, and punishes his mother.

All of these stories appear to be confused and illogical reworkings, reminiscences perhaps, of an originally clear plot. Every attempt to heighten the effect of the heroine's sufferings, through repetition of accusations or duplication of persecutors, simply results in a loss of logical sequence and probability. Nevertheless the central scheme begins to emerge with increasing clarity, despite all disfiguring variations. A number of European examples illustrate the most significant of these variations. A German story, for instance, substitutes the girl's own mother for a mother-in-law as persecutor;[33] other stories retain the King's mother as persecutor beside the girl's own mother, making her the victim of two women instead of one.[34] A confused tale of this type, beginning with the mother as persecutor but not clear in its later course, has been recorded by Jean Fleury.[35] A popular story from Italy[36] combines mother and mother-in-law as persecutors, and represents the two old women as working together. Another[37] lays the whole treason, both the initial persecution and the letter reporting the birth of monsters, to the account of the mother alone. A Sicilian story[38] deliberately contrasts the cruelty of the girl's proper mother with the tenderness and humanity of the King's mother. One detail of this last plot is remarkable, and deserves to be mentioned parenthetically. When the evil mother tampers with the first letter, she does not write in an accusation of an animal birth, but of infidelity on the part of the young queen. This accusation is so

[33] Heinrich Pröhle, *Kinder- und Volksmärchen*, Leipzig, 1853, no. 36.

[34] Christian Schneller, *Märchen und Sagen aus Wälschtirol*, Innsbruck, 1867, no. 50. Cf. Grimm, no. 31. Also I. and J. Zingerle, *Kinder- und Hausmärchen aus Süddeutschland*, Regensburg, 1854, 124.

[35] *Lit. Orale de la Basse-Normandie*, Paris, 1883, 151.

[36] Gherardo Nerucci, *Sessanta Novelle Popolari Montalesi*, Florence, 1880, 43.

[37] *Ibid.*, 134. The list could be extended, of course.

[38] Laura Gonzenbach, *Sicilianische Märchen*, Leipzig, 1870, no. 24. For bibliography, see Stanislao Prato, *Quattro Novelline*, Spoleto, 1880, 94 ff.

very rare in folk-tales—almost unheard of, in fact—that such an occurrence makes the rarity all the more striking.

We have not yet exhausted all the types of story which center about the more primitive accusation. As the preceding instances show, there are many reasons given for the exile, or for exile and handlessness, in which the King finds the heroine before he marries her and which—usually—expose her to the resentment of his mother. So far as any exile is mentioned at all, it has been explained by desire to escape a marriage with a monster, or persecution by a jealous mother. Here is a more edifying motive employed to reduce the girl to that condition of helplessness and mutilation which kings in folk-tales found so irresistible: [39]

A very poor couple have a daughter. One day a stranger stops at the hut, and offers to provide for the girl if they will surrender her to him completely after twelve years. The father consents, and espies the cloven hoof too late. At the end of twelve years, the Devil comes to claim her; but she has washed and crossed herself, and he has no power over her. To prevent this frustration of his plans a second time, he orders the greedy father to cut off her hands and lead her into the forest. Since she contrives to wash and cross herself before losing her hands, the Devil has no power over her, even in exile. The young King riding by sees her, and takes her home and marries her. While he is away at war, she bears twins. The messenger meets a witch whose evil glances change the letter into news of the birth of cats. The horrified King gives command to expose her in the forest again. When she tries to drink from a spring, one of her children falls into the water. Her hands are restored by her grasping after it with the stumps. She is harbored in a magic castle, and served by invisible hands. Meantime the King has "learned the truth" [how?], sets out to find her, and finally does so. He takes her home; and the magic castle vanishes.

A more coherent form of the same plot is summarized by de Puymaigre [40] from a Catalan story. Here again a father sells his daughter to the Devil, and her hands are cut off because she persists in nullifying the bargain by crossing herself. It is the same Devil, not an intruding witch, who changes the letters. This same economy of plot distinguishes the tale of *Das Mädchen ohne Hände* in Grimm. In a Lithuanian story, [41] the girl's fear of her

[39] Dietrich Jecklin, *Volkstümliches aus Graubünden*, Zürich, 1874, I, 111.
[40] *La Fille aux Mains Coupées, Revue de l'Histoire des Religions*, X, 193-209.
[41] August Schleicher, *Litauische Märchen*, Weimar, 1857, 20.

father is well founded, and her exile is well deserved, because she has killed one of his best servants. Several traits of this fairy tale recall *La Belle Hélène de Constantinople*, a medieval romance: the stealing of the young Queen's letter-seal by her mother-in-law, who writes that two puppies have been born; the Queen's hand tied around her child's neck; the stealing of the infants by an animal; the manner of recognition by means of the hand. The tale may indeed be descended directly from some consciously artistic narrative.

Other stories explain the first exile of the heroine by her father's irritation at her excessive piety, which provokes him into driving her forth handless. Such, for instance, is the motive in the Italian legend of Oliva.[42] The name of this heroine suggests a relationship with the medieval legend of Saint Olive, which was popular in Italy as a miracle play. A short story from Armagnac[43] concerns another heroine who suffers persecution, loss of her hands, and exile, because her father resents her devotion to the poor. The instigator of the father's actions is one of the ubiquitous stepmothers, so potent for evil in märchen. The story does not contain a royal marriage for the young exile, or accusations of an animal birth and a second exile. It simply restores her to her parish as quickly as possible, where her presence has a very desirable effect on the crops. It illustrates, incidentally, the separate existence of component parts of our more complicated type-tale, and makes clear that every handless girl does not necessarily marry a king's son, or go into exile because her father wants to marry her. The ingredients of the Exchanged Letter story exist separately; and in combination they show endless variation. This fact is a reminder of the hopelessness of tracing a folk-tale to a definite original home. One is led to posit an "Urtypus" as original ancestor; and then suddenly the figures of demons and witches and

---

[42] G. Nerucci, *Sessanta Novelle Popolari*, 324. See notes on Grimm, no. 31 (*Anmerkungen*, I, 295), *Das Mädchen ohne Hände*. One of the Arabian Nights is devoted to such a tale (ed. Burton, IV, 281-283). The girl's hands had been cut off because she violated a royal decree against almsgiving; the King marries her nevertheless; her jealous co-wives write to their husband that she has been unchaste. So she is exiled with her child, and her hands are restored when she reaches after them into the water.

[43] Jean François Blade, *Contes et Proverbes Populaires Recueillis en Armagnac*, Paris, 1867, 55.

cruel fathers and stepmothers begin to shift and merge into one another in the most bewildering fashion. Who shall undertake to decide between the merits of witch and stepmother as claimants to the rôle of original persecutor?[44]

A few words remain to be said about the stepmother, who has been hitherto neglected in this discussion. A fair example of her activities in the Exchanged Letter story may be found in Brittany:[45]

A man remarries, and his daughter by the first wife is badly treated by her stepmother. During his absence the unfortunate Euphrosine is left in a tree in the forest, handless. A young gentleman finds her, takes her home, and marries her. The affection of his mother towards her turns to hatred. While the husband of Euphrosine is absent, she bears twins. Her mother-in-law sends word to him that they are a dog and a calf. He replies that the animals are to be killed, but his wife must be spared. Instead, she is forced to go into exile a second time with her children strapped to her back. Her hands are restored to her when she reaches into magic water after her babies. Years later, the husband finds wife and children while he is hunting in the forest. He imprisons his mother in punishment.

Almost identical is the story of the fair Rosina from Italy,[46] except that her second exile takes the form of floating across the sea in a chest with her two children. The mother-in-law is not present in the castle when the children are born, but the messenger stays with her a night on each trip, and gives her each time an opportunity to change the letter. The brother of the absent King is the person who suggests that the Queen be set afloat instead of being killed then and there.

A Greek story[47] containing a stepmother is worthy of mention because it is another of the few which substitute an accusation of infidelity for an accusation of bearing animals. This fact, besides the general courtly and literary flavor of the plot (notice the use of a tournament, for instance, to bring characters together!) makes one doubt the popular nature of the story; but, whether or not it has been affected by self-conscious literature, it must be reckoned with:

[44] Cf. also Radloff, *Proben der Volkslit.*, IV, 408. Again the story stops with the first exile.
[45] Paul Sébillot, *Contes Populaires de la Haute-Bretagne*, Paris, 1880, I, 105.
[46] G. Nerucci, *Sessanta Novelle Popolari*, 348.
[47] Emile Legrand, *Recueil de Contes Populaires Grecs*, Paris, 1881, 241.

ACCUSED QUEENS IN FOLK-TALES 31

Princess Marie is deprived of her hands and driven into exile by her wicked stepmother. A King's son finds her, and, with his father's reluctant consent, marries her. Her husband goes to a tournament proclaimed by her father. There Marie's stepmother falls in love with him, and there he is supposed to receive news of the birth of two sons. But the stepmother intercepts the tender greetings that are to go back to Marie, and changes them to a command to kill her because she is of disgraceful origin and unfaithful. Her father-in-law exposes her instead. The Virgin restores her hands. Her husband, having heard his father's tale, seeks her and finds her. She divulges her identity, and goes with her husband to visit her father. The stepmother is burnt to death.[48]

This story appeared in the seventeenth century in a book called Ἡ τῶν ἁμαρτωλῶν σωτηρία[49] by a monk of Crete. The probability of literary connections is thus increased.

A rather restricted group presents still another personage as traitor and persecutor: namely, the wife of the heroine's brother. It is a familiar trait of fairy-tale heroes that they are unusually devoted to their sisters, and accompany them through the most trying adventures with witches and stepmothers. Sisters, too, commonly display a most admirable desire to free their brothers from inhuman shapes or inhuman behests. One is tempted to see in this devotion a distant trace of early matriarchal society, with its close dependence of a sister and her children upon her brother, which has left other marks as well on the constitution of conservative fairy-tale society. However that may be, the conflict between a man's sister and his wife underlies this interesting legend, which contains some additional material on the custom of infanticide in fairy tales.[50]

A father who has twelve children tries to rid himself of the two oldest by losing them in the forest. His second attempt succeeds. Brother and sister have an adventure with a forest witch. They escape from her together. In time, the brother marries an evil woman, who tries to ruin the innocent Jeanne, her sister-in-law. She kills her own child and accuses Jeanne of the crime. For some unfathomable reason Jeanne fails to defend herself. She is turned out of the house with both arms torn

---

[48] Cf. also Wuk Stephanowitsch Karadschitsch, *Volksmärchen der Serben*, Berlin, 1854, no. 33.

[49] *Le Salut des Pecheurs*, par Agapios de Crète, moine de Mont Athos, 1641.

See A. Ch. Gidel, *Études sur la Lit. Grecque Moderne*, Paris, 1866, 289.

[50] F. M. Luzel, *Légendes Chrétiennes de la Basse-Bretagne*, Paris, 1881, II, 235.

off by her brother. A nobleman finds her in the forest and marries her, in spite of her mutilation. While he is away at war, she bears twins. But the messenger passes the house of her wicked sister-in-law, who changes the letter to report "a cat and a dog," and the return letter to a command for the exile of all three.

Jeanne goes forth into exile once more. She finds asylum with the converted witch (who figured at the beginning of the story). Her father finds her here, with her arms restored by the witch. A belated explanation takes place on the part of the too-reticent Jeanne, and the wicked sister-in-law meets her deserved punishment.

A Russian parallel [51] omits the episode of the witch and the exposure of brother and sister by an unnatural father; but the sister-in-law plays the same part.

In a Finnish variant, the heroine again maintains an irrational silence in the face of her sister-in-law's accusation.[52] This time, the changer of the letter is an "evil woman," whose connection with the plot is not clear, and whose forgeries are repeated a bewildering number of times. Each time the children alone are exiled, whereupon the Devil takes them. After the fourth birth and treachery, the Queen herself, with the last infant, is set adrift on the sea. In the end, she is restored to her husband but not to her brother, who is apparently forgotten.

This family of stories, no matter how close their relationship, presents enough variety to widen considerably our knowledge of persecutors. Again it is to be noticed that no character similar to the villain Robbrecht has been cited, nor have I found any such in examining folk-tales. The accusation of infidelity is very seldom encountered. We move still in a world of frenetic family hostilities: hatred of stepmother for stepdaughter, mother for daughter, mother-in-law for daughter-in-law. The mother-in-law leads in numerical importance. She is usually the forger of lying letters.[53] One wonders why, of course. The hostility of an old queen towards her son's wife is not confined to this definite pattern märchen. It may be worth while to glance at a few instances outside of the Exchanged Letter cycle.

[51] August von Löwis of Menar, *Russische Volksmärchen*, Jena, 1921, no. 26.
[52] A. von Löwis of Menar, *Finnische Märchen*, 53.
[53] In an isolated instance, the loss of the mother-in-law as persecutor has left the burden of forgery to the messenger himself. His behavior is unmotivated; and the story would be incomprehensible without the other members of the cycle. (Klara Stroebe, *Nordische Volksmärchen*, I, 1.)

ACCUSED QUEENS IN FOLK-TALES 33

1. In Grimm's *Märchen* no. 49, *Die sechs Schwäne*, a sister redeems her brothers from raven's form by seven years of silence, during which she makes a magic shirt for each brother. Her mother-in-law takes advantage of the girl's supposed dumbness to expose her children successively, substituting animals.

2. A. de Gubernatis, *Florilegio delle Novelline Popolari* (Milan 1883) p. 306. A King's mother hates his young wife. During his absence at war she orders the young woman taken out into the woods and killed. Instead, the servitor blinds her and takes the eyes home. Her adventures end with restored sight for her and death for the dowager.

3. V. Imbriani, *La Novellaja Fiorentina*, 1844, p. 232. A King goes hunting. He unspells a fair lady in an enchanted castle, and marries her secretly. He says nothing to his mother, even when his wife bears children. But the old Queen finds out his secret, and attempts to destroy the family of her son.

4. Avenstrup and Treitel, *Isländische Märchen und Volkssagen*, Berlin, 1919, p. 24. Hildur is the young wife of the King of the Netherworld. She is loved by husband, children, and subjects; but her mother-in-law hates her and curses her, so that she is compelled to spend every day and night of the year on earth as a witch, except only Christmas Eve. The King pleads with his mother to remove the spells (p. 30): "Take back your curses, mother, and give ear to my prayers, so that my Queen need no longer remain far from me, and my joy at our meetings may last longer than it does now." She answers: "All of my curses shall be upon her still, and nothing will move me to recall them." Hildur is eventually unspelled by a bold mortal who witnesses these scenes under the protection of invisibility.

And so on.[54] It may be futile to look for an explanation for causeless hostilities in the bewitched world of fairy tales. The characters and motives in that world seem at first too topsy-turvy, too remote from rational sequence and reality, for satisfactory explanation. But the more one studies popular tales the more they reveal a logic of their own, even in the matter of family hostilities. And these family hostilities, it seems to me, turn quite clearly on the matriarchal arrangement of society which they imply. How many a princess, for instance, is surrounded by her father with all sorts of restrictions to prevent her marriage, because her husband, rather than her brother, is to be his successor (and displacer) on the throne! The list is well-nigh endless, and particularly inter-

---

[54] For a very interesting extra-European example, see Paul Hambruch, *Südseemärchen*, Jena, 1921, no. 23. The wrath of the mother-in-law is as fiendish as it is unprovoked; and it extends to her grandchildren as well.

esting in connection with Damiet and her father in *Esmoreit*. How many a tabu marriage, like that of Amor and Psyche, recalls matriarchal exogamy! And if we are justified in this interpretation, we may see in the secret marriage of the King in the third tale above, a strong reminiscence of the time when a man supported his mother and sister, while his wife remained elsewhere and was supported, along with her children, by her own family of brothers.[55] If this is true, it is easier to understand the hostility of the mother-in-law to any arrangement which might shift her son's allegiance and support from her own domicile to his wife's. One is tempted to say definitely that the mother-in-law got her traditional rôle assigned to her—a rôle perpetuated still in current jokes—during a time of transition from the one phase of family life to the other. The speech of the King of the Netherworld in the Icelandic tale[56] sounds very much like a plea for the change! Apparently not all human races went through just this evolution of domestic loyalties, or in just this order.[57] Many anthropologists believe that the order is as often reversed. But it seems to me that a large number of märchen, European and extra-European, bear traces of an origin among people who were living in such a transitional stage, when filial allegiance was beginning to shift toward marital allegiance. It is hard not to think so when one finds stories stating expressly that "The King became so fond of his wife that he neglected his mother, and she sat brooding revenge in her own castle"—or something of the sort. Her wrath and jealousy are a matter of tradition, then, even after the transition is complete. And she is still wrathful and jealous in medieval literature.

Because of these indications (proofs one can hardly call them), namely, numerical preponderance, and consonance with a demonstrable form of primitive society, I am inclined to select the mother-in-law as the most ancient persecutor. If an Urmärchen of the

[55] For interesting echoes of this condition in later literature, see W. O. Farnsworth, *Uncle and Nephew in the Old French Chansons de Geste*, New York, 1913; and A. W. Aron, *Traces of Matriarchy in Germanic Hero-Lore*, University of Wisconsin Series, 1920.

[56] No. 4 above.

[57] Robert H. Lowie argues strongly against the universality of such a sequence in *Primitive Society*, New York, 1920, Ch. IV.

Exchanged Letter type really existed as common ancestor of modern European ones, it might have run something like this:

A girl is exiled for some cause over which she has no control: her stepmother's jealousy, her sister-in-law's hatred, her father's cruelty, or a supernatural persecution. A King finds her, usually mutilated as to hands, and takes her home to marry her. His mother resents the marriage, and retires to her own castle. When the young Queen gives birth to children during the King's absence, the messenger is entertained by the old Queen, who changes the letter during his sleep to report the birth of animals. The King receives the letter and is properly horrified, but he nevertheless replies with a command to care for his wife tenderly. The old Queen changes this humane message into an order for the exile of mother and children, either in the forest or on the waters. Through supernatural aid (magic spring, grateful animals, fairies, etc.) the heroine's hands are restored and a house is provided for her. Here her husband discovers her, having brought to light the treason in the family by a few well-placed questions, and having punished his mother with a sufficiently barbarous death.

The innumerable variants of this hypothetical plot show how completely the people have made it their own. The most salient feature of it—the accusation of bearing animals—remains, however, surprisingly constant; and the figure of the mother-in-law is the motive power for evil in a majority of the stories. More we cannot say about the origin of the type.

One subdivision of the cycle, important for its affiliations in medieval literature, remains to be discussed. I refer to that group of stories which motivate the heroine's initial exile by the persecution of an incestuous father. Although that formula is important enough in literary versions which combine it with the Exchanged Letter, it is seldom employed in fairy tales as prologue to our plot. The few instances I have found seem clearly traceable to known medieval versions, and belong properly therefore in another chapter. Such, for instance, is the Italian "La Madre Oliva,"[58] which, by its very title, betrays descent from the medieval legend of that name:

A Queen, dying, exhorts her daughter to continue her work of alms-

[58] *Archivo per lo Studio delle Tradizioni Popolari,* Palermo, 1882, I, 520.

giving. [This seems to be a faint approach to the use of piety as a trait provoking paternal persecution.] One day the King sees his daughter, and remarks to her abruptly, "My daughter, I am in love." She asks innocently, "With whom, father?" "With your beautiful hands," he replies. She promptly cuts them off and sends them in a golden vessel to her father. He is much chagrined. To express his disapproval of her conduct, he sets her afloat over the sea in a chest. Near her landing place, she is found by a King who, of course, marries her. His mother disapproves strongly, and announces, "I shall retire to a monastery."

During the King's absence, the usual treason is perpetrated by the King's mother. The accusation is again the birth of animals. The second forgery demands the death of mother and children. Instead "they" cut off the hands of the young Queen [again!] and let her wander into the forest. She recovers hands and husband in the usual way.

In one story from Hesse given by Grimm in his notes, as a variant of the usual "Mädchen ohne Hände" type, the girl is again driven out handless by her father in the beginning, because he wanted to marry her.

Such is the order of events made familiar to us by poems of the Middle Ages like *Mai und Beaflor*. But it must be confessed that just this sequence is foreign to the folk-tales, except in a few suspiciously literary instances.[59] If the hypothetical author of the Urmärchen really began with the incest-motive (as is sometimes assumed), why has this opening formula been so universally replaced by others in contemporary versions recently collected? The question leads back to another one already raised: Is not the whole plot simply an accretion of separately existent independent formulas? But that query is merely interesting, not answerable.

It so happens that the formula of the incestuous father as persecutor does occur very frequently in märchen,[60] outside of the group we are now discussing. It is generally associated with the Cinderella heroine, who wins herself a prince as husband by her mysterious appearance at three successive balls in magically radiant gowns. A typical and conveniently elementary form is preserved in a Lithuanian tale:[61]

---

[59] Cf. Romanceiro, *Choix de Vieux Chants Portugais* (trans. by de Puymaigre), Paris, 1881, nos. 9 and 10, and the bibliographies of each. Cf. Däumling's Arabic tale mentioned on p. 26, n.

[60] For a tabulation of variants of this Cinderella tale see Marian Roalfe Cox, *Cinderella: Three Hundred and Forty Five Variants*, London, 1893, xxxii-xxxiii *et passim*.

[61] A. Leskien and K. Brugmann, *Litauische Volkslieder und Märchen*, Strassburg, 1882, no. 24.

A King loses his Queen, and can find no woman fair enough to marry after her—except his own daughter. She protests in vain; she spends the next night in tears. Her mother appears to her, and advises her to demand a dress of the sun as price of her consent. She obtains this from her father; also sun-gloves and sun-shoes; a moon-dress and a star-dress, and finally a complete coat of rat-skin. She puts on all her glorious raiment under the gray coat, and is carried away by her mother in a storm. Her father kills himself.

She finds herself near a rock, under which she hides the clothes. She appears as a rat to the King as he rides by. Because the rat can speak it is taken to the royal palace and given to a lackey as a curiosity. One day the lackey forgets to polish the King's shoes. The rat-girl does so and presents them to her master the King, who merely strikes her in reward. She follows him to church in her star-array, and dazzles him. When he asks whence she came, she says "From Shoe Castle." On another occasion she brings his knife to him at table, is struck by him for her pains, and follows him to church in moon-attire. This time she says she comes from Knife Castle. The third time she receives a blow when she fetches his forgotten handkerchief, and tells him in church that she comes from Handkerchief Castle. As she is leaving, one of her sun-shoes remains clinging in the tar that has been spread for the purpose. The King goes through the world searching for its owner, whom, of course, he eventually finds at home in the person of the despised rat-girl.

The second part of the story does not concern us here; but the first part, which is used as one means of getting our much harassed heroine into exile, most certainly does. It concerns us especially just because it does appear so often as part of another story. But it deserves to be considered separately, not merely as an introduction to the Exchanged Letter story.

In the Cinderella-cycle, the king's desire to marry his daughter is often based on a request of his dying wife. She bids him remarry only if he can find a woman whom her ring or clothes will fit. The king is unable to discover such a person until his daughter is grown; and then she accidentally proves her fitness for the honor by trying on the articles in question. In many stories the ring of her mother is the fatal object.[62] Other stories use the dead queen's

---

[62] A. de Gubernatis, *Tradizione Popolari de S. Stefano di Calcinaia*, no. 3; Isdem, *Florilegio delle Novelline Popolari*, 25 and 56; Gonzenbach, *Sicilianische Märchen*, no. 38; and the popular tale recorded by Straparola (Venice, 1567) in Favola 4. These versions are closely related, as their geographical distribution would indicate. The differences concern merely the exact nature of the magic dresses demanded by the heroine from her father (usually gowns of solar

clothes as a test for her successor.[63] One of these[64] uses the king-who-wants-to-marry-his-daughter to introduce an entirely different type of plot, resembling Danaë's story rather than Cinderella's.

In a few stories the queen makes her husband promise to marry only a woman more fair than she, and the fairer one is their own daughter. Such is the plot of *Le Taureau d'Or*, which has a second part different from the Exchanged Letter or the Cinderella ending:[65]

A King is happily married. After his wife's death and his promise about remarrying, he discovers that his daughter alone is more fair. He orders the wedding. The daughter, to delay it, asks him on her godmother's advice to get her a robe of the color of the sun; then one like the moon; finally a golden bull. She bribes the workmen to have the bull made hollow. She enters it secretly, and no one knows whither she has gone. Her father, now grown indifferent to the bull, sends it to a young Prince who is languishing for one. While the young man sleeps she steps out of it. One day he feigns sleep, and sees her. She restores him to health by giving him a new interest in life. She is married to him, and reconciled to her unnatural father.[66]

A similar legend is current in Germany to this day concerning Henry the Fowler and his daughter.[67] He wished to marry her after his wife's death because she was more beautiful. She begged him to relinquish his design, and he replied that he would if she would work a marvellous cover on which all animals could be seen. With the Devil's help, she accomplished her task, and her father died of chagrin. Other fathers give no reason for their

and lunar splendor, sometimes representing ocean and fields and sky: a sore temptation for a bit of nature interpretation!), the kind of disguise in which she escapes, and the exact method she uses to bedazzle the eyes of the prince she serves. But the outline remains firm and constant.

[63] J. F. Campbell, *Popular Tales of the West Highlands*, I, 226 (representing many others in which the girl's godmother advises her to demand the marvellous clothes); Auguste Dozon, *Contes Albanais*, 41 (noteworthy because the King's mother appears again as a subsidiary persecutor); Émile Legrand, *Recueil de Contes Populaires Grecs*, 217.

[64] H. and I. Naumann, *Isländische Märchen*, 221.

[65] Emmanuel Cosquin, *Contes Populaires de Lorraine*, I, 273.

[66] The escape in a chest and marriage with its next owner may be found in other tales: Straparola, Favola 4; Dozon, *Contes Albanais*, 41; a rather complicated narrative from Serbo-Croatia, no. 56, in A. Leskien's *Balkanmärchen* (Jena, 1919), and so forth.

[67] Kühn and Schwartz, *Norddeutsche Sagen*, 184.

strange demand.[68] One instance,[69] unique so far as I know, opens with a threatened incestuous marriage between brother and sister. The heroine goes into exile rather than carry out the wish of her dying parents, the King and Queen. Her other adventures are of the Cinderella-type.

Not only is the formula of the incestuous father *not* exclusively associated with one definite type of story like the Exchanged Letter or Cinderella (with which, as a matter of fact, it may have become associated by a kind of accretion, like the outer layer of a huge snow ball), but it sometimes exists quite alone or in other surroundings. In a group of märchen to which Stefanović first called attention,[70] the incestuous father not only causes his daughter's flight in the beginning, but pursues her later with persecution after she has married. In this case, as in the Offa story of the Middle Ages, he—instead of the mother-in-law—may be the person who changes the letter;[71] or he may substitute animals;[72] or he may kill his daughter's children and leave a bloody knife beside her to incriminate her.[73] If she is thus victimized by an accusation of child-murder, she is quite often driven into exile with the bodies of her children, and a miracle restores them to life before she is discovered and reclaimed by her husband. Here the use of the father on two occasions as a persecutor constitutes a gain in unity; the use of the bloody dagger suggests another popular story-group of the Middle Ages: the Crescentia-cycle. Radloff tells the Siberian legend of an ill-fated maiden whose father forced her to marry him;[74] and it is reported of the legendary Vortigern that he too married his daughter.[75] Perhaps a popular tale lurks behind this tradition, as with Henry the Fowler in modern Germany; perhaps something of the sort really happened. The question arises: why should a father appear in the guise of unnatural persecutor so often? And why, for that matter, is the same ungrateful function given so frequently to mothers-in-law in märchen?

---

[68] W. Webster, *Basque Legends*, London, 1877, 165; P. Sébillot, *Lit. Orale de la Haute-Bretagne*, 73; J. G. von Hahn, *Griechische und albanische Märchen*, Leipzig, 1864, no. 27, etc.

[69] A. von Löwis of Menar, *Russische Volksmärchen*, no. 9.

[70] Anglia, XXXV, 1912, 483-525.

[71] No. 6 (p. 498) of Stefanović's group: a Rumanian tale.

[72] *Ibid.*, no. 4.

[73] *Ibid.*, no. 6 *et passim*.

[74] *Proben der Volkslit. der türkischen Stämme Südsbiriens*, I, 190.

[75] Nennius, cap. 39; repeated by Henry of Huntingdon and Matthew of Paris.

C. Motivation of the Persecution

A comparison of modern folk-tales with certain classical myths will suggest an answer to the question about the reasons for paternal persecution in fairy tales. Hyginus, the classical Grimm (at least in respect to his zeal for recording popular tales, "fabulae"), lists a number of instances of father-daughter incest in connection with fable 253: Cinyras and Myrrha, Clymenus and Harpalyce (separately related in fable 206), Oenomaus and Hippodamia (fable 253), Erechtheus and Procris, Thyestes and his daughter (fable 87), Epopeus of Lesbos and Nyctimene (fable 204). In commenting on these and similar traditional occurrences, Sir James Frazer is led to inquire whether the stories may not have had an origin in some more rational, or at least pseudo-rational and understandable motive than a sensational and perverted imagination. The former assumption is more apt to lead to a satisfactory result, if one's aim is the philosophical attempt to harmonize facts and to discover a measurable order and causation in the study of fairy tales. Speaking of the ancestry of Adonis, whose father begot him on his own daughter Myrrha at a festival of the corn goddess, the author of *The Golden Bough* remarks that the multiplicity of such stories gives rise to the suspicion that the events (legendary or not) must be due to some cause other than an outburst of unnatural lust. He suggests this explanation:[76] "In countries where royal blood was traced through women only, and where consequently the king held office merely in virtue of his marriage with an hereditary princess, who was the real sovereign, it appears to have often happened that a prince married his own sister, the princess royal, in order to obtain with her hand the crown which otherwise would have gone to another man, perhaps a stranger.[77] May not the same rule of descent have furnished a motive for incest with a daughter? For it seems a natural corollary from such a rule that the king was bound to vacate the throne on the death of his wife, the queen, since he occupied it only by virtue of his marriage with her. When that marriage terminated, his

---

[76] *The Golden Bough*, IV, 44.
[77] Cf. Hyginus, fable 143, and the Russian tale mentioned on p. 39, note 69, and the innumerable fairy tales in which the royal crown actually does pass to "another man, a stranger," not of royal blood at all, who happens to win the princess.

right to the throne terminated with it, and passed at once to his daughter's husband. Hence, if the king desired to reign after his wife's death, the only way in which he could legitimately continue to do so was by marrying his daughter, and thus prolong through her the title which had formerly been his through her mother." As an illustration of the survival of this principle of descent, we are reminded that the Flamen Dialis in Rome was bound to vacate his priesthood at the death of his wife, the Flaminica.[78] Frazer does not suggest the group of European fairy tales we have just been considering as another illustrative survival, but the tales themselves surely offer a very close parallel to the customs he quotes. They are more convincing than the classical fables, because they more clearly center about a question of dynastic succession under a condition of matriarchy.

Matriarchy, or that system of human society in which descent is reckoned through the mother, exists or is traceable in several variations. In royal families, the successor to a king is often not his own son, but the husband of his daughter. The woman may not be the actual sovereign, but she confers the title on her consort *because she is her mother's daughter.* This family arrangement, however, shows signs of advancement towards patriarchy. In a still more primitive form, we are to imagine the mother and her children living without the father, while the place of protector is taken by the woman's brother. In a number of tribes, to this day, a husband does not live with his wife, but with his mother and sisters, only visiting his wife furtively. He supports his mother's family while he is continuing the family of his wife's brother.[79] So the kings in some of our folk-tales are at some pains to keep their marriages secret from their mothers, and the domiciles of the two women separate.

The Khasis of Assam are a living example of this arrangement. Children inherit through the mother only, and their father knows of no kinship with them. He belongs to his mother's clan as they do to theirs; what he earns goes to his own maternal stock. In Jowai, he neither lives nor eats in his wife's house, but visits it

---

[78] *The Golden Bough,* IV, 45.
[79] A very clear discussion (perhaps over-clear in that it invests a complicated subject with a too-geometrical simplicity, as if all institutions of all races had followed the same universal course) may be found in Edwin Sidney Hartland's *Primitive Society,* London, 1921.

only after dark. In ancestor worship, only the primal ancestress *and her brother* are regarded. Among the Pelew Islanders (Micronesian stock) a man's heirs are not his own children, but the children of his sister or his maternal aunt.[80] Before this arrangement had been established, the rôle of husband apparently did not exist at all. According to Mr. Hartland, the institution of matriarchy unquestionably goes back to a time when people were ignorant of the physical aspect of paternity.[81] To an uninformed and undeveloped mind, unable to span the lapse of almost a year between cause and effect, the relation of father to child might well remain unguessed. But the relation of mother to child is obvious and strong, and would logically form the central fact in the origins of family development. The social relations of primitive people point to great laxness, though not to absolute promiscuity, so far as we can judge; and this very laxness, prevailing as it does even among the extremely young, would be another cause tending to obscure the nature of paternity. "Whatever the exact course of evolution, the tie of kinship through the mother is that which meets us as most archaic in human societies."[82] This makes the transition to later forms of kinship seem more probable, since all forms of society are conditioned by what people know of themselves. "If mankind began by recognizing kinship with the father, the much more patent and undeniable relation with and through the mother must also have been recognized; how then could gentile kinship—kinship on one side only—have emerged? But if kinship with and through the mother was the primeval reckoning, though it might have taken generations or ages to pass through it, it is intelligible that kinship through the father might ultimately have arisen through the capture of women, the arrogance of conquerors, the overgrowth of clans or the decadence and dying out of clans. . . . That the course of evolution should have been reversed is inconceivable."[83] A number of illustrative examples could be quoted: matrilocal marriage among the Polynesians; matrilineal institutions among the Micronesians of the Pacific; matriarchy and

[80] *Golden Bough*, VI, 202-206.
[81] The märchen, of course, perpetuate this ancient ignorance in their endless tales of magic supernatural births without a father's agency; and the very accusation in the Exchanged Letter story, that the queen has borne animals, is another survival.
[82] E. S. Hartland, *op. cit.*, 36.
[83] *Ibid.*, 166 f.

traces of it among the Australians; the power of a maternal uncle over his sister and her children among the Fantis and the Bahuana of the Congo Basin; and the perceptible transition from mother-right to father-right on the Gold Coast of Africa. "Wherever we find a tribe wavering between female descent and male descent, we may be sure that it is in the act of passing from mother-kin to father-kin, and not in the reverse direction, since there are many motives[84] which induce men to exchange mother-kin for father-kin but none which induce them to exchange father-kin for mother-kin." [85]

Such is the reasoning of one entirely committed to the thesis that matriarchy must always have preceded patriarchy in the evolution of human society. On the other hand, many American anthropologists deny this necessity, and point out that the arguments in support of it are constructed *a priori*, without regard for examples of the reverse order of transition observed in contemporary primitive life. Perhaps English writers have been over-eager to make axiomatic statements and to reduce a very complex subject to a philosophic scheme.[86] The evidence of fairy tales may have a certain significance; and it so happens that the body of fairy tales concerning accused queens points to the precedence of matriarchy over patriarchy.[87] We have already met one indication of this precedence in the attitude of mothers-in-law towards their sons' wives, who threaten their dominance under the old family scheme. The Incestuous Father group seems to me to contain another such indication; but the following remarks are not to be understood as generalizations about all primitive human society. They apply merely to that society out of which grew the fairy tales now being discussed.

A difference in attitude towards incestuous marriages with relatives on the father's side and those with relatives on the mother's side is evident where paternity is the advancing institution. The

---

[84] Such as growing certainty of paternity, desire to have children inherit their father's property, etc.

[85] For material, see Edward Westermarck, *The History of Human Marriage*, London, 1891, Ch. XIV. The arguments there advanced are answered by Frazer, *Totemism and Exogamy*, IV, 92.

[86] Hartland's views are unquestioningly accepted by A. W. Aron, *Traces of Matriarchy in Germanic Hero-Lore*, University of Wisconsin Studies, 1920.

[87] Other groups might, of course, point to the reverse order. It would be worth while to investigate this possibility.

difference is of especial importance as a help in understanding the märchen type of the Incestuous Father. According to Mr. Hartland's reasoning, the story was possible partly because a daughter's relationship with her father was not always clearly realized, and then for a subsequent epoch it was not felt to be so strong as her relationship with the members of her mother's clan. Afterwards, when the prohibition of incestuous marriages is gaining ground among primitive people who are leaving matriarchy for patriarchy, it always extends first to the maternal side, while marriages with paternal relatives are long afterwards considered highly proper and respectable. The lowest stage may be found among the Kukis, where any marriage might occur except that of mother and son. Among the Karens of Tenasserin, alliances between brother and sister and father and daughter are still fairly common. The King of the Warua had in his harem sisters and daughters.[88] "Among the Wanyoro, brothers may marry their sisters, and even fathers their daughters, but a son does not marry his own mother, although the other widows of his father become his property."[89] As brother-sister marriages come to be looked upon as incestuous, a difference is made between the marriage with a half-sister who had the same mother, and one who had the same father. The former is often forbidden even when the latter is still permitted, as among the natives of Guatemala and Yucatan,[90] and in the royal family of the Banyoro in Africa.[91]

A definite connection apparently exists, therefore, between the transition from matriarchy to patriarchy, and the extension of the degrees of forbidden marriage to the father's side as well as the mother's. Both changes imply a growing consciousness of fatherhood as a basis of family organization. And they are both important for the understanding of that märchen formula so often used as an opening of the Exchanged Letter story, the Cinderella-story, and others. The story seems to have arisen among people who were passing into a clearer state of patriarchy from one in which matrilineal succession held good and in which marriage with a paternal relative was still possible. The king's desire to marry his daughter would then be comprehensible enough in the light of

---

[88] *Totemism and Exogamy*, IV, 132.
[89] *Ibid.*, 291.
[90] *Ibid.*, 295.
[91] Hartland, *Primitive Society*, 82.

obsolescent custom; and the marriage would be advisable as well as permissible for him if he wished to reign after his wife's death. The daughter's repugnance would be an index of the new and growing point of view. The conflict of the two, the old and the new, is thus incorporated dramatically in the tale. The story, having once originated under conditions so auspicious for a plot of conflicts (like the tales which preserve in dramatic form the conflict of a prince's loyalties to his mother, the older claimant, and to his wife, the newer claimant), continued to be told in its ancient outlines long after the cause of the escaping princess had been victorious, and father-daughter marriages had become a thing of the past. Hence the figure of the king merged into the vague horrible background of customs long disused and misunderstood but not yet forgotten; and the fading comprehension of his motives made him appear purely ogreish and monstrous. Yet one can sometimes detect a trace of the old restriction of succession which caused a king to seek marriage with his own daughter. Memories of it may explain the aversion of so many kings in folk-tales to the marriage of their daughters to any wooers whatsoever. The marriage would end the father's royal tenure, and his son-in-law would become his premature successor. Hence perhaps the manifold legends of princesses confined in windowless towers, kept away from the sight of men, or given in marriage only after their suitors have performed deeds of impossible difficulty to gain them. Hence tales like the classical myths of Atalanta and Hippodamia. It is interesting to recall that Apollodorus,[92] discussing the latter, suggests that her father's miserly attitude towards her suitors might be explained through fear of his son-in-law or a desire to marry her himself. The request of a dying queen in fairy tales and romance[93] that her successor should look like her, seems to be due to a distorted reminiscence of the time when she herself had constituted her husband's right and claim to the crown; and when it was perhaps necessary for him, in order to rule after her death, to marry one who could be regarded, in some mysterious way, as identical with her: either through resemblance, or daughterhood, or

---

[92] *Epitome*, II, 3, ff: Τοῦ δὲ βασιλεύοντος Πίσης Οἰνομάου θυγατέρα ἔχοντος Ἱπποδάμειαν, καὶ εἴτε αὐτῆς ἐρῶντος, ὥς τινες λέγουσιν, εἴτε χρησμὸν ἔχοντος τελευτῆσαι ὑπὸ τοῦ γήμοντος αὐτήν, οὐδεὶς αὐτὴν ἐλάμβανεν εἰς γυναῖκα.
[93] E.g., *La Manekine*.

ability to wear some token that magically transferred her personality to its pre-ordained wearer. And though the succession of kings in French romance is quite clearly patriarchal, traces of the old order lurk even in *La Manekine*, which begins with this familiar folk-tale situation.

One thing is sure about the system of marriage and succession which, in passing away, apparently gave rise to the story of the incestuous father. If matriarchy goes back to a time when the nature of paternity was not understood, it presupposes an original absence of jealousy on the part of husbands in matrilocal marriages: jealousy, that is, concerning the fatherhood of their children. Such is indeed the case among contemporary savage tribes. As Mr. Hartland says, with perhaps an over-dogmatic and unqualified positiveness: "It is clear that sexual jealousy plays a smaller part in savage life than in high civilization, and that where it occurs on the part of the man the danger of tainting the family descent does not generally enter into consideration. The truth is that the actual father is of no importance in these stages of society."[94] And curiously, we have found this condition to be true of the folk-tales, with their many reasons for exiling a heroine and persecuting her, apart from and exclusive of jealousy. The most striking result thus far has been negative. We have found very few accusations of infidelity, and no persecution arising from suspicious jealousy. We have followed the fortunes of heroines who go into exile or are otherwise persecuted because of jealous co-wives, insistent demon lovers, malevolent mothers-in-law, jealous mothers, incestuous fathers, impious fathers, and stepmothers. In this particular cycle, the accusation is almost universally a charge that the queen has borne animals instead of children;[95] and the persecutor seems for several reasons to have been originally the king's mother, who resents the transfer of her son's devotion to his wife (a change from the ideal matriarchal scheme). As for the king himself, he shows a conspicuous lack of resentment when he reads the forged letter,

---

[94] *Primitive Society*, 23.
[95] The bearing of animals might mean, to peoples who understood paternity and yet believed in the possibility of such births, a very gross form of infidelity (as in the Pasiphaë story) rather than witchcraft or animal nature in the mother. But the märchen which use animal parturition *as an accusation* seem to ignore this possibility. At least they show no interest in the question of fatherhood.

and he almost invariably sends back a command to guard his wife tenderly until his return. Evidently a royal husband was not expected to feel so much indignation if his wife bore puppies, as did the husband in the first group, where she supposedly killed or ate her children. Such at least is the situation to be found in folktales; and it is nicely in accord with Mr. Hartland's statement about the absence of jealousy in regard to the fatherhood of the children—even if, as one suspects in some versions, their father is supposed to be an animal.

D. Other Märchen Types

The discussion of the Exchanged Letter story and its motivation has led us far afield. The digression, however, is not without importance, since the motives discovered in the course of it will appear again and again in the stories still to be considered, both popular and literary.

There are a few remaining groups of märchen in which a queen is accused of crimes by a persecutor. In one of these, she is again accused of bearing animals. As one might expect, the identity of accusation with that in the Exchanged Letter cycle has caused, in certain instances, a merging of the two plots. An example of the mixed type will serve to introduce the new group:[96]

A peasant girl named Marie, whose fortune it is to marry the King of France, has an envious sister. The latter sends news to the King, during his absence, that his wife has borne a dog. The same treason is repeated the next year, and likewise the third year. At last the King orders that his wife be confined in a "basse fosse"—not, be it noted, sent into exile. Meantime the three children have been successively exposed by the jealous sister and reared by the hermit who found them. When the three (two boys and a girl) are old enough, they leave their fosterfather, taking a magic ring he gives them. They live with a kind old woman. The wishing ring helps them to prosper. One day the two brothers are turned into stone during an ill-fated visit to a fairy's castle. The kind old woman (really the Virgin) directs Marie in unspelling her brothers. The fairy becomes their friend.

One day the King sees his children. He is very much impressed by his daughter's power through the ring, and wants to marry her. But the princess-fairy reveals their relationship; the wronged Queen is liberated

[96] F. M. Luzel, *Légendes Chrétiennes de la Basse-Bretagne*, II, 274.

to die in peace; and the King marries the fairy princess, and puts the wicked sister of the first wife to death.

A second tale of this type introduces the quest of the two brothers of the heroine for a talking bird, a singing tree, and dancing water; but it retains from another source the mother-in-law instead of the envious sister as the cause of evil.[97] A convenient version to represent the story in its uncontaminated form is contained in the supplement to the *Thousand and One Nights*,[98] where the plot is worked out in great detail. Stripped of its elaborate descriptions and its polished courtly dialogues, the outline is reduced to this:

A Persian King wanders through the city by night with his Vizir, and hears three sisters making wishes. The oldest says she should like to marry the King's baker; the second prefers the King's cook; and the third says she should like to marry the King himself. If she were his consort, she would bear him a son with gold and silver hair, and pearl tears. The listening monarch decides to satisfy these wishes. The two older sisters are incensed at the good luck of the younger one, and decide to cause her ruin. They remain with her when she bears her first child; and, in place of the promised wonder-prince, they substitute a dead puppy. The King is annoyed, but his Vizir reminds him that the young Sultana is not responsible for Nature's freaks, and she is spared. The second year a "cat" is born, and the Vizir has difficulty in calming his prince; the third year the sisters announce the arrival of a "piece of wood." At this, the Sultan flares up in anger, and pronounces the death sentence over his wife. At the intercession of his advisers, this is changed into a fate cruel enough: she is walled into a space at the door of the chief mosque, and every Moslem who passes is compelled to spit in her face on pain of instant punishment.

Meantime the three real children have been exposed by the envious sisters. They are discovered and adopted by the court gardener, who leaves them at his death a beautiful estate in the country. One day a strange woman visits them, and tells the sister about the speaking bird, singing tree, and dancing water. (She is not an emissary of the envious sisters, as in so many European tales: she merely chances to mention the magic objects.) As usual, the brothers succumb to the perils of the quest, and are unspelled by their more successful sister. The wonders are brought home.

One day while the King is hunting, he encounters the two brothers.

---

[97] V. Imbriani, *La Novelaja Fiorentina*, 104.

[98] Burton, *Supplemental Arabian Nights*, IV, 491. This story was first introduced to Europe by Galland in the eighteenth century; but his Arabic source has not yet been discovered.

He is entertained by them and their sister. When, according to the advice of the speaking bird, he is served with pearl-filled gurkins, he exclaims in astonishment, "One can't eat pearls!" The bird replies: "Yet you believe that your consort bore a cat, a dog, and a piece of wood." It then tells the whole story of treason and deception. The Sultan orders the culprits tortured and killed, and the Queen is restored after her years of unspeakable agony.

Other Oriental tales, more recently collected, present variations of some importance. In an Arabian tale current in modern Egypt,[99] the quests are instigated by a woman sent by the envious sisters; the brother undertakes all three quests, and is uniformly successful; the fairy owner of the talking rose, whom he wins as bride, tells him and his sister of their ancestry. In a Bengal story, six childless jealous co-wives do the substituting of puppies in place of the promised wonder children; the recognition is brought about as in the Egyptian tale. A Buddhist legend[100] is constructed on a simpler formula. The Queen, formerly a destitute girl, is envied by the other wives. When her twin children are born, they cover her eyes, cast the infants into the river, and smear her face with blood. They accuse her of *having eaten her two sons*, and she is condemned to death. A wise man at court learns the truth through a heaven-sent dream; the children are restored—after exposure and adoption—because of their striking resemblance to the King. The quests are entirely lacking. As for the accusation of cannibalism brought against the Queen, it is not at all unique, though it is not usual in this cycle. We have encountered it frequently elsewhere. Smearing with blood may be a more primitive device than substituting animals, but we cannot judge with certainty.

The European parallels to this tale are very numerous and very faithful to its structure.[101] Bolte and Polívka point out that the uniformity of all versions and the logical sequence of the complicated plot indicate a single source unknown to us. In only one detail do the European fairy tales improve on the logic of events

---

[99] G. Spitta Bey, *Contes Arabes Modernes*, Paris, 1883; summary in Clouston's notes to Burton's *Supplemental Arabian Nights*, IV, 619.

[100] Mitra, *Sanskrit Buddhist Literature* of Nepal, Calcutta, 1882, 65-66. Summary by Clouston, *op. cit.*, 647.

[101] A bibliography of them will be found in the notes of Bolte and Polívka to Grimm, Märchen 96, *Anmerkungen*, II, 380.

in the Oriental version. They motivate the desire of the young princess for the three magical objects through the report of them, not from a chance visitor, but from the envious sisters who wish to destroy her.

The European versions of this tale run more true to type than the variants of the Exchanged Letter story. It will be convenient and legitimate in this case to construct a composite märchen from, say, twenty typical examples. The following will be used and referred to by number. Important variations are noted in parentheses.

1. E. Cosquin, *Contes Populaires de la Lorraine*, I, 186.
2. T. F. Crane, *Italian Popular Tales*, New York, 1885, p. 17.
3. J. Curtin, *Myths and Folktales of the Russians*, London, 1890, p. 517.
4. A. Dirr, *Kaukasische Märchen*, Jena, 1920, no. 9.
5. A. Dozon, *Contes Albanais*, p. 7.
6. L. Gonzenbach, *Sicilianische Märchen*, no. 5.
7. A. de Gubernatis, *Florilegio delle Novelline Popolari*, p. 309.
8. *Ibid.*, p. 315.
9. J. G. von Hahn, *Griechische und albanische Märchen*, no. 69.
10. V. Imbriani, *La Novellaja Fiorentina*, p. 81.
11. *Ibid.*, p. 114.
12. P. Kretschmer, *Neugriechische Märchen*, Jena, 1919, p. 257.
13. I. Kúnos, *Turkische Volksmärchen*, p. 63.
14. E. Legrand, *Recueil de Contes Populaires Grecs*, p. 77.
15. A. Leskien, *Balkanmärchen*, no. 57.
16. C. Mijatovies, *Serbian Folk-Lore*, p. 238.
17. H. Pröhle, *Kinder- und Volksmärchen*, no. 3.
18. C. Schneller, *Märchen und Sagen aus Wälschtirol*, no. 26.
19. W. Webster, *Basque Tales*, p. 176.
20. P. Zaunert, *Deutsche Märchen seit Grimm*, Jena, 1919, p. 141.

A King has a habit of wandering about his city at night and listening to conversations. (He has forbidden the use of lights after dark: 5, 10, 13, 14.) He overhears three girls (whose poverty forces them to spin by moonlight, 6; or to disobey, 13, 14) boasting or making wishes about marriage. The eldest and second wish to be married to the King's cook and baker (or chamberlain and butler); but the youngest (the second, 16) boasts that if she were Queen she would bear marvellous children (with golden stars on their foreheads, or golden hair, or some such royal sign). (In 17, 20, the King overhears them in the fields; in 4, in the royal stables; in 18, in their father's castle. In 5, 15, 16, all three sisters are boasting what they would do if they were married to the King; and in 5, 15, he grants their wish. In 10, the remarks are overheard by the King's cook and reported.) The King satisfies the sisters' desires. The youngest becomes Queen, to the annoyance of the other two (of the King's mother, 1, 9, 10; his stepmother, 16; the King's mother and the two sisters, 14; the King's own sisters, 10).

(The opening formula is omitted in 1 and replaced by another in 4.) The young Queen bears children as marvellous as she had foretold (in the King's absence, 1, 2, 5, 6, 9, 10, 15, 16, 18, 19. In several of these the persecutors send letters bearing the false tidings; in 16, for instance, the letter of the King's mother openly accuses the Queen of familiarity with goblins). At these births—successive or simultaneous— the envious sisters contrive to substitute animals. They tell the King that these are the offspring of their sister. He believes them, and orders that the Queen be imprisoned in a dungeon, or half buried in the earth near the palace (e.g. 13), or sent to a treadmill.

Meantime the children have been exposed, usually on a river, by the envious sisters (in 1, by order of the King himself). They are rescued and reared by a kind person. When they are grown up, the King sees them and yearns over them instinctively. (In 1, 2, 7, the boy has a quarrel with his foster-brother, learns that he is a foundling from a taunt that is hurled at him,[102] and sets out with his sister to find his parents.) He returns home and tells his sisters-in-law (or mother), who guess the truth and plan to ruin the children. So they put a desire for the speaking bird, singing tree, and dancing water into the head of the young princess. She asks her brothers to get them for her. (4, 11, 16, 20 omit the quests entirely, to the detriment of the plot; 10, 18, 19 have the quests suggested by a chance remark, as in the Arabian Nights.) The three wonderful objects are finally obtained, often, however, only after the brothers have failed and the sister has come to their rescue. The King invites the young people to his palace. At dinner, the truth-speaking bird tells the story of the children and their mother (or the fairy who replaces the bird does this in 5, 13, 14, 15. In 6, the children had disobeyed the royal decree that all passers should spit on the Queen). She is recalled from her prison or living grave and placed beside her husband once more. The envious sisters (mother-in-law) are executed, and all ends well.

The plot is unusually coherent and constant in these twenty versions. And these versions were not chosen for the sake of their uniformity: rather the reverse. The action is fairly complicated also; and the envious sisters are the persecutors in nearly all tales.

---

[102] This is a common device for revealing his status to the hero in romances also: cf. *Seghelijn van Jerusalem* and the legends of the medieval Gregorius-cycle.

The plot is therefore more unified and economical than in the Exchanged Letter story, where a separate persecutor is provided in each exile of the heroine, except in the group where the incestuous father later brings about an accusation of child-murder. The European fairy tales are even more unified than the Arabian legend, because they use the same envious sisters to motivate the quests. If the story goes back to a single (Oriental) original, the work of a single artistic mind, it probably contained this deft weaving also. The probability that the source was Oriental is increased by two considerations: first, the fact that the King is discovered walking about the streets of his city at night incognito, a habit much affected by mythical eastern potentates; and second, that in several of the versions listed, the King marries all three of the sisters, singling the youngest out to be his favorite.

Again, however, the story is interesting and important as popular literature, even if it does go back to a single original. In the first place, it has been, like the Exchanged Letter story, the subject of many substitutions and modifications which testify to its popularity and its nearness to the sources of märchen formulae, with their manifold persecutors. From these sources of popular imaginative tradition came the substitutions recorded above. In the second place, this unified, comparatively artistic plot, perhaps self-consciously created, is after all only a mosaic of motifs quite familiar in other fairy tales. The accusation itself, which is the chief concern here, is the old one of an animal birth, so widely and firmly believed to be possible by all sorts of primitive folk. The story of the Zulus has already been quoted (p. 27) in which several of these motifs have been combined independently into a similar mosaic: the birth of the monster (this time real, not the result of substitution); the exposure; the disgrace of the wife at the village gate in a solitary hut; the appearance of the children who have issued out of the monster; the reinstatement of the wife through the action of her children. The human offspring are very often exposed on a river, as in many a venerable legend of the Romans or Hebrews or Assyrians. They are in several cases suckled by wild beasts. The adventure of the perilous quest is worked out in formulae readily identified by the seasoned reader of märchen. For instance, in the Arabian as in several European versions, the brothers in turn leave a life-token with their sister when they depart: a knife which becomes rusty or drips blood when its owner has met an evil fate. A wealth of parallels to this use of the life-token has been collected by Mr. Hartland in the second volume of his study on the Legend of Perseus. The device is certainly not an exclusive invention of the clever young sister in this tale. In the third volume of the same work there is much said, besides, about the petrifaction of heroes in the course of a difficult adventure, and how the heroes are later unspelled by a more successful comer, when magic water is sprinkled upon them. Such is the order of the enchantment and disenchantment here. Both the life-tokens and the release from petrifaction can be reduced to terms of sympathetic magic. Certainly, as ingredients of a story, they are no invention of the hypothetical author of the Urmärchen about the Envious Sisters. They were used by oral story-tellers everywhere. The very behavior of the children when they discover that they are foundlings resembles that of many others recorded and discussed in M. A. Potter's *Sohrab and Rustem*,[103] where the changing status of a foundling is definitely connected with the changing status of marriage.

The family of stories which goes by the name of the Envious Sisters is composed, therefore, of elements not always the same in all individual versions, but all very familiar in märchen literature. As in the Exchanged Letter cycle, we have found a certain divergence of treatment of the motives and personality of the persecutor, who may be the mother-in-law or King's sisters or King's stepmother. But in this cycle, as in the preceding one, the Queen is still accused universally of an animal birth; the charge of infidelity is still foreign to her in popular literature,[104] and the figure of the ambitious villain is still entirely without prototype in fairy tales. One feature of the Envious Sisters plot does reappear in medieval romances like the Swan Knight story. That feature is the imprisonment of the accused queen until her children come to rescue her. This is an important substitution for the exile of the queen. In medieval romance, it is equally popular, though it awkwardly delays the queen's restoration until her children's return many years later. Hence the embarrassment of a long interval

---

[103] London, 1902.   [104] See p. 46, n. 95.

between the first part of the action and the second, and a consequent weakness in such plots as *Esmoreit*.

Queens in exile are popular in their own right in fairy tales, whether or not the exile is caused by an accusation. If it is not, the ladies are not interesting to us here, except for the sake of instructive comparison and the satisfaction of observing how exile and distress are motivated without marital jealousy. The breaking of a tabu is frequently used. This brings us of course to the domain of Amor and Psyche, into which I have neither the temerity nor (fortunately) the need to enter. But that universal and infinitely varied tale may at least be mentioned. In it, a heroine is married to a supernatural or non-human husband (often a creature of double nature, man by night and animal by day), whom she is forbidden to see or mention to others, or whom she must not know by name. When she breaks the tabu and penetrates her husband's mystery, he often disappears and leaves her to search for him through years of painful wandering, until she has worn out several pairs of iron shoes and endured the sight of witches and monsters and the marriage of her husband to another woman, before she is restored to him once more. Thus, in fairy tales, the breaking of a prescription or a tabu is a great crime against marriage. But it is still not infidelity, and no accuser is involved.

Another cause of exile is the persecution of a young princess by an interloper when she is about to be married, or just after she has been married. This type of story is called the Substituted Bride.[105] It, too, requires only a passing mention, because it contains no accuser; but, since it does contain a persecutor, it deserves the quotation of a few examples. Perhaps two will suffice; and since they are chosen from countries so widely separated as Iceland and the Malay Peninsula, the wide diffusion of the tale is sufficiently apparent.

This is the Icelandic märchen:[106]

A prince named Sigurd goes to a distant land, wins a royal wife, and shares the government with his father-in-law. When he hears of his father's death, he sets sail for home with his wife and child. One day,

---

[105] For discussion and bibliography, see P. Arfert, *Das Motiv von der unterschobenen Braut in der internationalen Erzählungsliteratur*, Schwerin, 1897.
[106] Hans and Ida Naumann, *Isländische Märchen*, no. 24.

when the Queen is alone on the fore deck, a stone boat comes up alongside. Out of this astonishing vessel a grim giantess emerges. She steps over to the Queen, bespells her, changes semblance and clothes with her, and takes her place. The helpless Queen is placed in the stone boat, which is put under the behest that it keep going until it reaches the brother of the giantess in the underworld.

The giantess attempts to take the Queen's place, but her demon-like nature asserts itself. The King is puzzled; his domestic peace is quite destroyed; the child cannot endure its changeling mother. Meantime the Queen has fallen into the power of the underworld giant, who gives her a chance to be restored to her husband. He permits her to appear ghost-like in Sigurd's palace on three successive nights. The first time she says, "Twice more will I come, then never again." The last time, fortunately, the King is present and embraces his wife. She is thus regained from the other world, and the giantess is compelled to return to her brother's regions.

The Malay story:[107]

A Prince carries off a Princess and her maid as his booty. He intends to marry the Princess in his own country. During the voyage, the maid seizes an opportunity to cast her mistress overboard and usurp her place. The Prince accepts her. The unfortunate Princess grasps the keel of the vessel and is dragged through many a weary mile of ocean until the ship reaches shore. A fish bites out her eyes, but still she does not relax her hold until the end. She bears a son in solitude. The child grows up and becomes the means of restoring his mother completely to her former estate. First he catches the fish with her eyes in it, and gets a medicine man to restore them to her head. Then he draws the King's attention by the gold star on his forehead—an infallible sign of royalty—and he asks to have his mother invited to the palace. Here her tale is heard and she is restored.

In some tales, it is the daughter of the scheming nurse of the princess who is substituted.[108] The formula, being popular, shows many variations; but it is fairly constant in development everywhere. Sometimes it is used at the end of stories which originally had nothing to do with it.[109] A prince, returning with the unspelled princess whom he has won by perilous adventuring, is some-

---

[107] Paul Hambruch, *Malaiische Märchen*, no. 45.

[108] In a tale from Epirus (von Hahn, *Griechische und albanische Märchen*, no. 31), we have a stepmother's daughter as substituted bride.

[109] E.g., the story of the three love-oranges; see *Folk Lore Journal*, VII, 1889, 85.

times rash enough to leave her by a fountain while he goes ahead to prepare a fitting welcome for her in the palace of his parents. An ugly slave or a jealous or ambitious servant passes by, forces the princess to change clothes, throws her into the water, and attempts to impersonate the bride herself, saying that the sudden change in her complexion is due to exposure to the sun while she waited. The prince, with the obtuseness which characterizes fairy-tale monarchs when injustice is being done against their rightful wives, takes the miserable substitute with a barely expressed gesture of doubt, and the marriage is broken only when the real bride manages to make herself known. The story-type is not important here, but it reminds us once more that, with all the possibilities for causing an innocent queen's exile, the motive of marital jealousy is generally ignored. And the restoration of the wronged queen through the agency of her son (as in the Malay version), proves again that the fundamental structure of *Esmoreit* is not peculiar to that play, nor to medieval literature in general.

One more reason for the persecution of innocent ladies is sure to impress the curious reader of fairy tales. The persecution again arises, as in the incest-formula, from the girl's father; and once more the cause is fundamentally fear: fear of the girl's husband, his successor. In the one case, the father had tried to avoid his doom (loss of his throne to his son-in-law) by becoming his own successor and son-in-law. In the present case, the father tries to avoid doom at the hands of son-in-law or grandson[110] by jealously guarding his daughter in an attempt to prevent her marriage. Often she is secluded like Danaë, in a high, inaccessible tower. When a supernatural lover makes his way to her, often in the guise of a bird, and she bears a child in spite of her father's anxious precautions, then exile and suffering frequently follow for mother and child alike. In this way, the fate of the persecuted queen is combined with that of the exposed child.

A few summaries of stories which open with the Danaë situation, more or less similar to the classical legend of the birth of Perseus, will serve to recall the prevalence of the type.

1. L. Gonzenbach, *Sicilianische Märchen*, no. 27. A prophet, passing a princess, shakes his head and foretells a dire fate for her at the age

---

[110] Cf. the story of the exposure of Cyrus, as told by Herodotus, I, 107 ff.

of eleven. So the King her father has her shut up in a high, windowless tower. One day she rubs a hole in the wall, and a man-bird flies in. He becomes her lover; her father's precautions have been in vain. Cf. also *Ibid.*, no. 45.

2. *Ibid.*, no. 28. It is prophesied that a princess will bear a child to the sun. The girl is confined in a windowless tower. She scratches a hole in the wall with a piece of bone; a ray of the sun shines upon her, and she is made a mother in accordance with the prophecy. Here the child alone is exposed.

3. A. and A. Schott, *Walachische Märchen*, Stuttgart, 1845, p. 262. A maiden is condemned to seclusion in a tower, far away from men. But one day she eats a flower that a gypsy had given her, and, as a result, finds herself pregnant. Her father sternly casts her afloat in a cask, where she bears her son.

4. F. S. Krauss, *Sagen und Märchen der Südslaven*, Leipzig, 1883-1884, I, 195. A girl is innocently made pregnant by a plot of the Queen mother, because of the latter's jealousy at the King's love for his daughter. She and her son are set afloat on a ship by the irate monarch.

5. J. Curtin, *Myths and Folktales of the Russians*, p. 47. A Tsar's daughter is confined in a high room, far from the sight of men. When she is grown up, they allow her to walk out one day, and a terrible Whirlwind abducts her. She is rescued by her youngest brother.

6. M. Wardrop, *Georgian Fairy Tales*, London, 1894, p. 25. A King builds a tower in which his daughter is to be guarded as a protection against marriage. One day an apple comes floating across the water to the tower. She and her maid eat of it and become pregnant. The King indignantly orders the death of both of them; but the servitor entrusted with the task of execution spares them instead, and leaves them to their own devices in the forest.

7. L. Gonzenbach, *Sicilianische Märchen*, no. 16. A young hero has an adventure of the Amor and Psyche sort with a fairy mistress, with the rôles reversed. Here it is the man who must suffer and search before he can regain his supernatural mate. Among other things, he must release her from the power of her father's spirit, which exerts a baleful influence to prevent her marrying.

8. K. Stroebe, *Nordische Volksmärchen*, I, no. 30. A Princess looks out of her window one day and laughs at a ridiculously lazy fellow named Lars who is passing by. When she cries, "You ought to have a boy" (to help him in the work he so heartily detests), he replies, "You ought to have one too." And since he has the power of obtaining anything he wishes, he actually fathers a child on the Princess by his words. The King is exceedingly angry. When the child is old enough, he gives the boy an apple and bids him give it to his father. The child unhesitatingly presents it to Lars. The King is angrier than ever, and sets all three adrift in a boat. They reach an island. Here the Princess, having learned of her husband's wishing-gift, causes him to employ his power in build-

ing her a castle and in reforming himself. So all ends happily; the old King himself is finally reconciled, and Lars is recognized by him.

This story is closely paralleled in other versions: e.g., F. M. Luzel, *Légendes Chrétiennes de la Basse-Bretagne*, I, 59; and von Hahn, *Griechische und albanische Märchen*, no. 8. In the latter, however, the King cannot bring himself to recognize the hero as his son-in-law even at the end. A fainter replica of the situation appears in Avenstrup and Treitel, *Isländische Märchen und Volkssagen*, p. 7. Here the child is not of magic origin.

It might be suspected, from the point of view of our modern patriarchal society, that the king persecutes his daughter when she bears a fatherless child, simply because she has brought disgrace on the royal family and he is ashamed of her.[111] But this does not explain the initial fear, which leads him to guard her so jealously. Prophecies are no explanation, because they simply raise the question, "Why the prophecies themselves?" The situation might remain incomprehensible were it not for the stories in which kings surround the wooing of their daughters with other difficulties than the penetration of a closed tower: perilous quests, riddles to be answered, contests to be won, and so forth. The number of kings who say, "You may not marry my daughter unless you do thus-and-so," is legion; and their obvious purpose is to prevent the marriage of the princess. If we begin to inquire into the reason for this paternal aversion to a daughter's marriage, we soon come upon the explanation suggested for the story of the king who wants to marry his daughter. The monarch fears his daughter's husband because he sees in him his own successor. Under strict matriarchal succession, the son-in-law would assume the prerogatives of kingship upon his marriage with the princess, without waiting for her father's death. The crown would be his in virtue of his marriage with her, just as it belonged to her father by virtue of his marriage with her mother. Certainly the explanation seems inherent in the nature of a story which, for another reason, bears traces of origin under a matriarchal society.

That other reason is the manner of the birth of the princess's son in the Danaë type of legend. In the examples just quoted, and in many more that might be mentioned, the heroine is made

---

[111] Such is indeed the case in a tale like Gonzenbach's 87th, which has a late and Christian coloring, in spite of the supernatural birth of the hero from a virgin.

a mother in a most singular way: by eating an apple or a flower; by allowing a ray of sunlight to fall on her (how close, this, to the shower of gold in the orthodox classical myth!); by a bird; by the mere wish of a passer-by. In number 5, the heroine is rescued by her younger brother, who is born in consequence of his mother's having swallowed a pea. Now we have already noticed that matriarchy is not only characterized but perhaps conditioned and caused by such an ignorance of the nature of paternity as these stories imply. It is unthinkable that people retrograded from a true knowledge of human geniture to a fantastic belief in the fertilizing powers[112] of an apple, a flower, or a pea. And since so many of the Danaë stories are constructed on the theory of a hero's birth without a human father, I think we may fairly assume that such surely belong, if any do, to a very early stratum of folklore deposit; and that their origin dates back to an age which knew matriarchal descent alone because motherhood was the only form of parenthood about which people had a clear notion. In such an age, under such a society, a growing comprehension of a father's relationship to his children might well exist side by side with older beliefs about the conception of children. The two exist side by side in the Danaë tale. The old king knows well enough that the princess is his daughter; but he finds it not at all surprising that she should be doomed to bear a child to the sun.

Through tangled and dim old paths, overgrown with the underbrush of ancient and terrible beliefs, we have been led far afield in the search for an answer to the question, "Why are queens in folk-tales accused?" At times, it may have seemed that the path was exceedingly faint, the traces obliterated, the tortuous bending of the trail without a goal. The research could indeed have been infinitely extended; for customs and beliefs merge into one another and overlap so imperceptibly that one can take any single instance —sympathetic magic, life-tokens, child-sacrifice—as a point of departure for an excursion through the whole endless field. Even this miniature inquiry has been threatened from time to time with confusion and bemazement in the labyrinth of primitive superstition. Nevertheless a few facts of importance have emerged.

[112] For a bewildering array of such beliefs, see Hartland's *Legend of Perseus*, London, 1894.

The figure of an innocent and persecuted queen who is later restored to her rights and dignity, is not confined to medieval romance. She meets us frequently in folk-tales. The crimes of which she stands falsely accused in these tales are various; and no matter how impossible or unnatural they may seem to us, no matter how urgently they seem to demand incredulity on her husband's part, they are usually accepted by him as possible and even probable. These crimes and accusations become more significant when compared with customs and beliefs current among so-called primitive peoples to-day. We have found our persecuted heroines accused of infanticide: a crime not only still comprehensible but also still widely practised in certain parts of the world. Moreover, the crime itself appears (not merely the accusation of it) in many popular tales which give as reasons for it the reasons which evidently still hold good where infanticide is now practised. Other accusations include bearing animals, which is again a subject of sober belief among people who do not understand clearly the nature of paternity or who still believe in witchcraft and in the existence of men with animal natures; the breaking of a tabu (which might have deflected us into an endless pursuit of parallels and causes); and witchcraft. The persecution results from the plotting of such typical persecutors as the royal mother-in-law, with her ancient inherited hostility to the young wife who shares her son's affections; the torture inflicted by a supernatural being who has obtained a certain right over the heroine (by contract with her father, or unsatisfied demand for sacrifice, or by changing shapes and clothes with her, as in the Substituted Bride tale); the exile or confinement or both caused by a father who fears his successor. When the heroine's father does the persecuting, he seems to be actuated by fear: a fear which leads him to seek incestuous marriage with his own daughter or to prevent her marrying anyone else (he surrounds the wooing of her with insurmountable difficulties, or else confines her in an inaccessible tower).

But of all the causes examined, the one most conspicuously absent is a husband's jealousy. It is present only in two of the tales cited; and those are naturally only a very small part of the number previously examined for the purpose of this study. The absence of this motive agrees with the comparative absence of jealousy—jealousy in behalf of the family honor, though not necessarily in the desire for ownership—among people living in a state of matriarchy. The evidence for the origin of our fairy tales under such a state has been gathered from other internal evidence: that ignorance of paternity so often referred to; strong traces of matrilocal marriage; the frequency with which a märchen king recognizes his daughter's successful wooer as his successor, even if the happy youth is only a gardener's son or a Dümmling.

So it seems quite likely that innocent persecuted queens were popular long before narrators thought of attaching to them so modern an accusation as infidelity. In fact, they must have been popular before such an accusation was possible or conceivable. And for the same reason, the earliest heroines are never persecuted by a personage like Robbrecht, a relative of the credulous king, a scheming villain who hopes to be the next occupant of the throne. His rôle also is unthinkable in the more primitive tales which we have analyzed, because the succession to the throne is provided for in quite another way. Instead of a villain, we have stepmothers and mothers-in-law and witches, and fathers who are cruel because their fear is great. These figures are surely more truly "primitive" and popular than is the polished courtly traitor who does evil for the sake of his ambition. I do not mean to reduce the whole problem to a ridiculous simplicity by the statement of a dogma like this:

A mother-in-law is a more primitive persecutor than an ambitious nephew; and

The bearing of animals is a more primitive accusation than infidelity;

but some such priority does become probable in the light of the märchen we have examined. It means that the accusation brought against a queen like Hermione in *A Winter's Tale*—more credible to others though perhaps no more horrible to her than the fantastic ghoulish accusations of the fairy tales—is a comparatively late arrival in popular literature: late, at least, as the institution of patriarchy, which it implies, is late in comparison with the institution which preceded it. But it is time now to examine the literature of this later period, so far as it affects the sorrowful persecuted Queen of Sicily, or Chaucer's heroine in the *Man of Law's Tale*.

CHAPTER III

THE ACCUSED QUEEN IN ROMANCE: FOLK-TALE SURVIVALS

VARIOUS cycles of medieval fiction are devoted primarily to the sympathetic treatment of accused queens, who are as popular in romance as in märchen. Often, indeed, the authors of romances wrote with real pathos and indignant partisanship concerning the misfortunes of their exiled heroines; often, too, they emphasized the sorrows of innocence with such delight that they transgressed the limits of artistic good taste and fell into sentimental lachrymosity. But at least there is never any doubt of their sympathies. The persecuted lady is still the victim of malice and false accusation; the husband is still credulous; and the vindication is often brought about by the grown children of the royal pair, as it was commonly in folk-tales. Other elements in the plot are, however, transformed. The accuser and the accusation particularly undergo a most interesting change. In certain stories, the persecutor who disturbs the happiness of the royal household appears in one of the guises already familiar to us in märchen: as a stepmother, a sorceress, or a mother-in-law. The accusation which blasts the innocent heroine is, in this type of story, one of the fantastic charges already noticed in the preceding chapter, and harmonizes perfectly with the folk-tale character of the person who utters it. The supposed offense which causes imprisonment or exile is still archaic and unbelievable to us: witchcraft, familiarity with demons, giving birth to animals. In other words, a certain number of medieval romances are built on a plot which, told in summary, would pass easily as the plot of a naïve folk-tale, no matter how richly the story-teller has overlaid his simple structure with the ornaments of romantic fiction. The cycles of Constance and of the Swan Children are good examples of such plots.

In another group, however (Chapter IV), a significant change is apparent. The traditional persecutor still holds her place very prominently; but beside her appears a new figure, entirely foreign to the folk-tales. It is a co-persecutor, a man who aids in undoing his liege lady because of some special hatred. Sometimes the old mother-in-law so dominates the action still that she completely overshadows this new person, whose motives for hating his queen are not explained. When his motives *are* revealed, they usually hinge on rejected love. This is a new grievance, so far as this study is concerned. No persecutor thus far has turned vindictively upon a fairy-tale queen for just this reason. With the emergence of this persecutor the motivation becomes more romantic.

In a third cycle of stories (Chapter V), the romantic persecutor, a courtier-villain, has entirely replaced the mother-in-law of the märchen-plot. He works alone. His motive is either ambition to advance himself and his family at the queen's expense, or, again, a desire to enjoy revenge for rejected love. His hostility is more readily explained than was that of the old mother-in-law, and is certainly more comprehensible to us. Moreover, his accusation has been changed to accord with his new surroundings, now very different from the matriarchic society of folk-tales. He does not, as did the evil-speaking mother-in-law, assume that witchcraft and the bearing of animals are the most heinous of crimes; he tries rather to ruin the queen by declaring that she has committed adultery or been guilty of high treason.

Of course, many romances of the first group, such as Chaucer's *Man of Law's Tale*, are just as late in time of composition as some romances of the last group. But individual stories of the second group, where the two types of motivation exist side by side, indicate that we have to deal with a real development of the mechanism of the plot from one phase to another. Certain stories of this second group, such as *Valentine and Nameless*, exist in two forms, an older and a later one; and these two forms show decisively that it is the mother-in-law who is the waning figure, and the villainous courtier who is developing. The latter must therefore have been better adapted to the general development of romantic plots in the Middle Ages. He remains the favored character for the initiation of villainy for many centuries to come.

Beginning with the first group of stories, in which there is no trace of a rejected lover or an ambitious courtier, we find a number of formulae from folk-tales. One of the most striking instances of this is the use of the Incestuous Father as a means of getting a persecuted heroine into exile for the first time. But whereas this device is most often used in märchen to introduce a Cinderella-story, with the dazzling appearance of the heroine on three successive occasions in her magic gowns, the Incestuous Father formula in the literature of the Middle Ages is generally used to introduce an Exchanged Letter story, and the accompanying accusation of bearing animals. There is no trace of the Cinderella-conclusion in any of the popular medieval representatives of the story we are investigating. The opening, however, is strikingly like the folk-tales. A king's wife dies, to his great grief; he remains disconsolate for years, refusing to marry; finally, when his daughter is grown up, he yields to the importunity of his court and consents to take another wife if one can be found exactly resembling the first. Of course his daughter alone fulfils the condition. A struggle of wills ensues, from which the daughter emerges triumphant—but an exile. When she flees from her father's realm, she has often sacrificed one or both of her hands in an attempt to render herself unfit for the marriage (by becoming unlike her mother), or because the offending members were especially attractive to her father. Later she finds refuge in the household of a king who determines to marry her, in spite of his mother's hostility towards the nameless, handless fugitive. So far the prelude in all versions is quite constant, except in treatments like Chaucer's, which show deliberate change to avoid the incest-motive. The logic of events is generally the same, and the action is frequently localized in England.

Gough[1] has attempted, chiefly on the basis of this constant opening formula, to disentangle, as source for the first part of the medieval Constance-legend, a single hypothetical Anglian folk-tale, which he infers from the existence of many other folk-tales throughout Europe. Both he and Suchier[2] justly remark that, since the oldest version (*Vitae Duorum Offarum*) appears in England, and since several other versions (*La Belle Hélène de Constantinople*, and those by Trivet, Büheler, Chaucer, etc.) use England as the scene of the action, therefore England has the strongest

---

[1] A. B. Gough, *The Constance-Saga*, Berlin, 1902.

[2] Edition of *La Manekine* for the Soc. des An. Textes Fr., I, lxxiii-lxxix.

claim to the origin of the underlying folk-tale. "While endeavoring to determine the primitive form of the saga," says Gough, "we must not neglect the numerous folk-tales, scattered over nearly the whole of Europe, which contain the same story in varying forms. Most of these are probably unaffected by the literary versions . . . and reach back to a remote antiquity." He does not give his reasons for attributing great antiquity to the tale. Moreover, it seems to me that these correspondences and similarities indicate only that the Incestuous Father tale was early united with a version of the Exchanged Letter tale—and not, by any means, to the most common version of it—in England, but not necessarily in England alone. It is not impossible that the former story existed independently elsewhere, since, as we have seen, it has parallels in classical mythology and in popular custom. To track an elusive folk-tale back to a supposed definite source in time or space, is an impossible task. Suchier[3] had already pointed out before Gough that the Constance-saga is a composite of two well-known types: the Peau d' Âne (Incestuous Father plus Cinderella), and a general cycle of persecuted women. So much has been made clear by the examination of fairy tales in the preceding chapter. It is not necessary to assume definitely that the Peau d' Âne story existed only in Anglia before the Conquest, though an Anglian version may well have been predominantly important for succeeding literary products. In this discussion, there will be little attempt to construct genealogical tables for the relations of popular stories. And our chief interest in the literary stories is not their relations and interdependence so much as their deviations in the introduction of new motives for the persecution of queens.

Since the Latin narrative attributed to Matthew of Paris is the oldest in time, it has a claim to first treatment, even though, as is apparent, it is one of the least faithful in observing the general plot which is typical and persistent in the Middle Ages. The story is found in the *Vitae Duorum Offarum*,[4] and is usually dated in the later twelfth or early thirteenth century.[5] The monarch of

---

[3] *Ibid.*, lxxix.
[4] Contained in: *Matthaei Paris Historia Major et Duorum Offarum Merciorum Regum*, Wil. Wats, London, 1684.
[5] F. Holthausen, *Beowulf*, Heidelberg, 1919, note to line 1931.—Wats, *op. cit.*, 965 ff.—Edith Rickert, *The Old English Offa Saga*, Mod. Phil., II, 2.—R. W. Chambers, *Introduction to the Study of Beowulf*, Cambridge, 1921, 36-37.

whom the tale is told must really have reigned on the continent, before the coming of the Anglo-Saxons to England. He is here, however, represented as a Mercian king.

One day, while Offa is out hunting, he hears a sound of tears and lamenting. He finds a beautiful girl who looks like a princess, alone in the forest. She tells him that a great calamity has befallen her "because of her sins," and that she is "Reguli cuiusdam filia qui Eboracensibus praeerat." This King, inflamed with love for his own daughter, had tried to move her with threats and persuasions and to "weaken the constancy of the girl with bribes." She had remained firm; "Cum pater tamen minas minis exaggeraret, promissa promissis accumularet, munera muneribus adaugeret" [like the insistent fathers in fairy tales], she had preferred exposure or death to yielding. Her father had ordered her to be killed in the forest, but the assassins had left her alive instead.

Offa takes the maiden home. When he is urged by his nobles to marry, he decides to take no one else. The marriage is duly celebrated.

Years later Offa goes to a war in which he is victorious. A messenger is sent home with the good tidings, but evil fortune takes him to the castle of the King of York, father of the heroine. The King learns of the posture of affairs and uses his opportunity. He gives the messenger an inebriating drink, opens his letter, and changes it to a report of calamity in war. The blame for the defeat is laid on the King's young wife, who is accused of witchcraft. In punishment, she is to be exposed in a desert place, "ubi cum pueris suis puerpera, truncata manus & pedes, exemplo pereat inaudito." The agents of death accordingly cut her children to pieces, but they spare her for her beauty. A hermit hears the sounds of woe from the mother, follows them, beholds the cruel sight, prays, and restores the reassembled children to life. He cares for the desolate exiles.

Offa, returning home after two months, asks questions about his wife. The evidence of treason is revealed, and he is disconsolate. His courtiers advise him to seek distraction in the hunt. Of course, he meets the worthy hermit, tells his tale, and is happily reunited to the family.[6]

So once more the incestuous father appears as initial cause of the heroine's exile in an Exchanged Letter tale. But the curious thing about this story is the double rôle played by the father. As in Stefanović's group of folk-tales, the father has taken over the function of writer of false messages, and has thus brought about an organic unity between the two portions of the fable. Other

---

[6] Concerning the probability that Matthew of Paris did not write the *Vitae*, see Suchier in *Paul und Braune's Beiträge*, IV, 500-521.

romances, however, do not show a similar narrative economy. The *Vita* in which Offa is associated with an Accused Queen may therefore be regarded as an offshoot from the direct line of development of the legend in the Middle Ages. It can be neither direct ancestor nor direct descendant of any other known medieval version. It became modified, perhaps, in being associated with Offa; or perhaps a different märchen background explains it. How the tradition came to be attached to Offa is another question, probably unanswerable. It is instructive at least to remember the figure of Henry the Fowler as he lives in German tradition.[7]

Much has been written about the tales clustering around Offa and his Queen. There is enough obscurity in the matter to give rise to many interesting, even plausible theories. The references to Offa and his Queen in *Beowulf*[8] are obscure; the relation of Offa I to Offa II is obscure, in so far as tradition, at work on both of them, tends to merge their figures and duplicate their tales; the relation of the real Queen of Offa II to the innocent persecuted Queen of legend is also obscure. The best that can be said of most explanations of the attachment of a Constance-story to the royal Anglian family is that they are interesting possibilities. Inconclusive, for instance, is the suggestion that Drida, heroine of the second of the two *Vitae* and consort of Offa II, is also an exiled princess fleeing from an unnatural father, just because it is said in Beowulf that she crossed the water *be fæder lāre*, and brought jewels enough with her to deserve the epithet *goldhroden*. As Miss Rickert says,[9] "The expression *be fæder lāre* is as easily explained to mean that she went at her father's bidding (perhaps with him) as that he sent her into exile."[10] The utmost that can be assumed for the Drida-story, as it is told in the *Vita Offae II*, is that it looks like a representative of the general Danaë type, with the added peculiarity that its heroine is marked by a ferocious temper characteristic of some other Germanic maidens, so that she is anything but an unmixed blessing to the hero who marries her. The suggestion of Miss Rickert that Drida (or Petronilla, as the *Vita* also calls her) may be equated with Berta the daughter of

[9] *Mod. Phil.*, II, 340.
[8] L. 1931 ff.
[9] *Mod. Phil.*, II, 340.

[10] An ingenious explanation is suggested by R. C. Boer, *Handelingen van het derde Nederlandsche Philologen-Congres gehouden te Groningen*, 1902, 84-95.

Charlemagne, is again merely a suggestion which leads nowhere.[11] Miss Rickert concludes that "all these hints point towards the inference that some form of the *Berte* legend (Petronilla being derived either by corruption or wilful variation) has influenced the text of *V 1*"—namely, the story summarized above concerning Offa I. It is unavailing to conjecture further on such remote possibilities.

This much, at least, is clear: a narrative composed of the Exchanged Letter plus the Incestuous Father formula appears in England in the late twelfth or early thirteenth century; and this narrative probably does not represent a typical form of the story because it stands alone in its modification of the plot, especially since this modification may be a conscious artistic improvement to bring the two halves of the plot into closer organic connection. It seems necessary, therefore, to postulate a still earlier date for the emergence of the Constance-story in England in a shape similar to that preserved in most medieval versions (i.e., with a persecuting mother-in-law in the second half). Holthausen states the matter thus: "We are concerned in this story, *Vit. Of. I*, with a variant of what is told in *Beowulf* of Offa and Þryð; the changes are to be explained by a mixture of the old tradition with legendary material about Cyneþryð, the consort of Offa II of Mercia, 758-96." The question of the degree of "mixture" could be disputed; but at least we have the product, and our task here is a comparison with other literary versions and with fairy tales—not with scraps of history which may or may not have had something to do with the tale before the Constance-legend influenced it. As for Drida, that enigmatical bad-tempered lady who drifted across the sea in the Latin *Vita* to become the destructive bride of Offa II, and who corresponds to the Þryð of *Beowulf*, bride of the continental King Offa I, centuries before, it will be best to leave her entirely out of the discussion. She has caused as much trouble among scholars of to-day as she did at her husband's court long ago; and we may congratulate ourselves that, since no mother-in-law drove her into exile from her husband's side, she does not concern us here.

Having begun with the oldest version, which happens to be the least orthodox, we must proceed to later medieval treatments, which

---

[11] See R. W. Chambers, *Introduction to the Study of Beowulf*, for a clear summary of the problem.

are truer to type. Of these, there are over twenty known at present. Most of these romances[12] in French, English, Latin, German,

[12] They are:

a. *La Belle Hélène de Constantinople,* MSS. in Paris, Arras, and Lyon. Summary in *Mess. des Sciences Hist. et Archives des Arts de Belgique,* Ghent, 1846, 169-209. A prose recension of the poem by Jean Wauquelin (1448) is contained in MS. 9967 of the Bibl. Royale, Brussels. Many folk-books were derived from this romance later. See Appendix II, no. 1; also R. Ruths, *Die fr. Fassungen . . . der Belle Hélène,* Greifswald, 1897.

b. *Mai und Beaflor,* Leipzig, 1848. A romance in the Austro-Bavarian dialect, dated by Suchier in the thirteenth century.

c. *La Manekine* by Phillipe de Remi, Sire de Beaumanoir, Paris, 1884. Written ca. 1270. A prose version of the poem by Jean Wauquelin is published in this edition, II, 267-366.

d. *Jansen Enikel's* story of the daughter of the King of Russia, l. 26678 ff. of his *Weltchronik.* Published by the Gesellschaft für deutsche Geschichtskunde, Hanover and Leipzig, 1900.

e. *La Comtesse d'Anjou* by Jehan Maillart. Composed in 1316. Summaries in: P. Paris, *Les Manuscrits Français de la Bibliothèque du Roi,* V, 42; A. d'Ancona, *Sacre Rappresentazioni dei Secoli XIV, XV, XVI,* Florence, 1872. Ed. *Romanisches Museum,* I, Greifswald, 1920.

f. *Fabula romanensis de rege Francorum, cujus nomen reticetur, qui in filia sua adulterium & incestum committere voluit.* In the Bibl. Nat. in Paris; written 1370. Cf. Ritson, *Ancient English Metrical Romances,* London, 1802, III, 324.

g. *Historia del Rey de Hungria,* a Catalan tale of the fourteenth century; summarized by Suchier, *La Manekine,* I, xlii; published in *Documentos Literarios en Antiqua Lingua Catalana,* Barcelona, 1857. See Däumling, *Das Mädchen ohne Hände,* Munich, 1912, 39 ff.

h. *Ystoria Regis Franchorum et Fille in qua Adulterium Comitere Voluit,* ed. Suchier, *Romania,* XXXIX, 61-76. Fourteenth century. [This proves to be identical with version "f" above.]

i. *De Alixandre, Roy de Hongrie, qui voulut espouser sa fille.* Published in *Nouvelles Françaises inedites du Quinzième Siècle,* ed. E. Langlois, Paris, 1908, 61-67.

j. *Il Pecorone* by Giovanni Fiorentino, tenth day, first tale.

k. Büheler's *Königstochter von Frankreich,* edited by J. F. L. T. Merzdorf, Oldenburg, 1867. The text is based on editions of 1500; Büheler wrote in 1401.

l. *Novella della Figlia del Re di Dacia,* ed. A. Wesselofsky, Pisa, 1866. The date of composition is uncertain, but it may well be much earlier than the date of the MS. (fifteenth century).

m. *Emare,* A Middle English romance of the fourteenth century. Edited by A. B. Gough, London, 1901; also for the EETS by Edith Rickert, 1908.

n. Italian *Oliva* stories, contained in the poem *Regina Oliva* and the play *Santa Oliva.* See *Revue de l'Histoire des Religions,* X, 197 f.; and d'Ancona, *Sacre Rappresentazioni dei Secoli XIV, XV, XVI,* Florence, 1872.

o. A French miracle play, no. 37, in *Miracles de Nostre Dame,* ed. Soc. des An. Textes Fr.

p. *Yde et Olive,* a continuation of *Huon de Bordeaux,* published in *Ausgaben und Abhandlungen aus dem Gebiete der romanischen Philologie,* LXXX, 152 ff.

q. *Herzog Herpin,* ed. in Karl Simrock's series *Die deutschen Volksbücher,* XI, 408 ff. Based on an unedited *chanson de geste, Lion de Bourges,* MSS. in Bibl. Nat., Paris. Fonds Fr. 22, 555 contains the pertinent episode, fol. 144b ff.; no. 351 omits it.

and Spanish begin with the flight of the heroine from her father to avoid an incestuous marriage, and conclude with her adventures as a persecuted wife, victim of a mother-in-law who tampers with royal mail and forges accusations under the royal seal. The three closely related versions[13] by Nicolas Trivet, John Gower, and Geoffrey Chaucer, substitute another formula in the beginning to replace the Incestuous Father. This form of the story is best known, because it was adopted by Chaucer. It retains the second formula, that of the Exchanged Letters, as faithfully as the others, from which it diverges at first.

These stories differ as did the fairy tales in explaining the father's conduct in the opening situation.[14] Sometimes a reason is given, and sometimes not. Most interesting are those romances which imply that the real difficulty arises from the attempts of the king or his barons to prevent the succession of the young princess and her future husband. The barons are determined that their king shall have a male heir; the king will not marry again, or will marry only his wife's second self; and so the choice is narrowed down to the incestuous union of father and daughter as an escape from female succession. In the entertaining romance of *La Belle Hélène de Constantinople*, for instance, the heroine is the granddaughter of the Emperor Richars of Rome. "Et nauoit cestui empereur nul hoir masle senon une seule fille laquelle estoit une tresplaisant damoiselle."[15] This damoiselle becomes Empress of Constantinople and dies in her turn, leaving, again, only a daughter

r. Bartolommeo Fazio's *De Origine Belli inter Gallos et Britannos Historia*, ed. Camusat, Bibliotheca Ciaconii, Amsterdam and Leipzig, 1744, cols. 893-902. Late fifteenth century. See Wesselofsky's edition of g, appendix ii; also *Cinderella* by Marian R. Cox, lxiii f.

s. *Le Victorial*, chronicle of Don Pedro Nino, by Gutierre Diaz de Gamez, 1379-1449. Translated into French by de Circourt and de Puymaigre, Paris, 1867. The pertinent passage occurs in Bk. II, Ch. XXVI.

t. *Columpnarium*, MS. Lat. 8163 of the Bibl. Nat., fourteenth century. Summarized by Edith Rickert in her introduction to *Emare*, xxxiii ff. It is a play which endeavors to treat the theme in a classical manner, with pseudo-classical names.

[13] Nicolas Trivet's Anglo-Norman *Life of Constance*, Chaucer Soc. Pub., London, 1872; Chaucer's *Man of Law's Tale*; Gower's *Confessio Amantis*, ed. R. Pauli, London, 1857, I, 179 ff.

[14] Suchier and Gough classify the stories according as the heroine is led into the forest for her second exile (the märchen setting), or drifts across the ocean, usually to Rome (more literary). The distinction is useful elsewhere, but is not relevant to the present purpose. Besides, the same distinction could be made as to the methods of motivating the first exile.

[15] MS. fol. 9b (prose version).

Hélène. The Emperor of Constantinople is exceedingly distressed. He turns with intensified affection to his daughter; and the author invokes the devil to explain the change of his affection into passion when Hélène is grown, instead of using a promise of the King to Hélène's mother. There follow the usual stormy scenes, the appeal of the father for a papal dispensation, and the flight of the princess. In the Middle High German *Mai und Beaflor*, similarly, the father's inconsolable grief for his Queen prepares the way for his unnatural passion for his daughter years later. The author is careful to explain that Beaflor was reared away from her father's sight, so that her sudden appearance before him in complete adult beauty and resemblance to her mother makes plausible his change of feeling. In *La Comtesse d'Anjou*, the father simply falls in love with his daughter one day while he is playing chess with her; in the *Historia del Rey de Hungria* the beauty of her hands inflames his love. In *Alixandre* the French prose states simply, "Le roy, pour la beaute d'elle, en fut si amoureaux que oster n'en pouit son cuer." So he issues a decree to legitimize their marriage. Her resistance to this decree causes him to set her adrift in a boat with her maid. She is handless because, having learned that her father loved her hands especially, she has cut them off and sent them to him.[16] In *La Figlia del Re di Dacia* the devil is once more blamed for the unholy passion which drives the heroine forth: "Lo re, tantato del nimico, villamente comincio a baciare lei, e oltre a questo le mise le mani in seno e 'n piu disonesto luogo; onde costei si vergogno molto di cio che 'l padre avea fatto."[17] Hence she is bidden in a dream to cut off the disgraced hand. In the Middle English *Emare* as in *Mai und Beaflor* the heroine is reared away from her father, after her mother's death at her birth. No explanation but her beauty is given for her father's changed attitude.

Other versions state explicitly that it is the girl's resemblance

---

[16] This prominence of the girl's hands as a love-inducing feature seems to be late. It comes about apparently as a rationalization of forms of the story in which she enters upon one or another of her exiles handless, as "La fille aux mains coupées." Sometimes the hands are cut off as punishment for her stubbornness in resisting her father; sometimes, as in *La Manekine*, their loss is a voluntary act of self-mutilation. If we may trust the evidence of the fairy tales, we should deduce that the hands were originally cut off as tokens to prove that she had really been put to death as her persecutor commanded. Fairy tales are full of such mutilations for the sake of evidence.

[17] P. 3.

to her dead mother which suggests to her father the idea of marriage. Thus in the *Victorial* the father and daughter mourn together, and he tells her that he should die if he did not have her, with her resemblance to her mother, as his comfort. Later his love changes and he wishes to marry her, saying that he cannot bring himself to marry one unlike his first wife. He kisses her hands; therefore she commands a trusty servitor to cut them off. In *Yde et Olive* the excessive grief of the father is again used to prepare us for the astounding decision to marry his daughter "pour lamour de sa mere," whom she closely resembles. But Yde flees the next day, disguised as a man; and her further adventures here and in the corresponding miracle play include her difficulties when she is expected to marry the daughter of an Emperor. In the romance, she is conveniently transformed into a man; in the play, the Emperor, when the truth becomes known, marries her himself. Both solutions are popular enough and can be paralleled elsewhere. They have nothing to do, however, with persecuted ladies.

More interesting still are the versions in which the royal father is urged to marry or decides to marry thus on account of the succession to the throne, with or without a limiting tabu imposed by his dead wife. These stories bring us into the region of the problems of the fairy tales. In the famous romance *La Manekine*, for instance, the King of Hungary promises his dying wife to marry only her double in looks and beauty. The wording of her request shows some reason for exacting it:

> 129 Sire je vous requier et proi
> Que vous ja mais femme après moi
> Ne voelliés prendre a nes un jor.
> Et si li prince et li contour
> De ce pais ne voelent mie
> Que li roialmes de Hongrie
> Demeurt a ma fille après vous
> Anchois vos requierent que vous
> Vous mariës pour fil avoir,
> Bien vous otroi, se vous avoir
> Poës femme de mon sanlant. . . .

He promises; and when his daughter Joie is grown, she alone fulfills the requirement. The barons begin to urge a second marriage;

he tells of his contract with the dead Queen; and after messengers have returned unsuccessful from a quest for her like among other princesses, it is the barons who suggest the incestuous marriage, urged on by Joie's own squire. Then comes the dispensation of the Pope; Joie's heroic attempt to disqualify herself by cutting off her hand (for no king in "Hongarie" is supposed to marry a woman who lacks any member), and her drifting across the sea in a little boat. Here the nobles of the court must bear most of the blame. The King succumbs to passion only after they had suggested the marriage. And in the narratives derived from *La Manekine* the responsibility is also placed on the dying Queen and the barons.[18] In the chronicle of Fazio, the situation is much the same. The dying wife begs her husband, Edward of Britain, "ne quam, ea mortua, uxorem induceret, quae non genere & forma par esset, quod quidem postulatum eo pertinere videbatur, ut rex memoriam ejus cum charitate perpetuo retineret; quum sibi persuaserat Regem nunquam inventurum, quae sibi his duobus ornamentis responderet."[19] Her motive is a simple desire to prevent entirely the King's remarriage. In time, the matter of succession begins to worry the nobles, and they implore him to marry "that he may leave behind him an heir of the male sex, to reign after him." While messengers are abroad searching for the bride, he falls into his ill-starred passion for his daughter. "Stimulabat eum virginis decor, matri aequalis," —but no special mention is made of her hands. Her flight follows inevitably. In *Columpnarium*, also, the dying Queen persuades Emolphus to marry only someone similar to herself; and hence his daughter is obliged to flee with her nurse Phocis, by sea.

Other romances made no reference to a definite promise, but they introduce the condition that the second wife must resemble the first. In the prolix romance of Büheler and in the Olivestories, the King imposes the condition voluntarily, for sentimental reasons; in Enikel's account, the King tells his barons he will marry only a woman who resembles his *daughter*, or, finally, only his daughter herself. The girl tries to avoid the marriage by cut-

---

[18] In *Herzog Herpin*, the nobles urge the marriage "damit er Erbe gewänne und das Land nicht an Fröhlich seine einzige Tochter fiele." The girl cuts off her hand in order that she may become unlike her mother—another ingenious rationalization of her lack of hands. "Meine Mutter hatte alle ihre Glieder," she announces; "ich aber nicht" (409).

[19] Cols. 893-894.

ting off her hair and scratching her face until she is "den tiuvel gelîch." She is set afloat in a vessel, richly dressed. The splendor of her garments here and in *Mai und Beaflor* and *Emare* recalls the series of supernatural robes obtained by the heroines of folk-tales from their fathers.[20]

It is evident that tradition was not uniform in accounting for the strange desire of the heroine's father to marry her. The oldest medieval instances, *Offa I* and *La Belle Hélène*, like many succeeding stories, simply state the fact baldly; others like *La Manekine* and its group use the device so insistently employed in the fairy tales, a promise to the dying Queen, with or without the advice of the barons of the realm; others use the striking similarity of mother and daughter. The daughter's resemblance to her mother reminds us, indeed, of the talismans used in folk-tales: a ring or an article of clothing which only the dying queen's successor can wear—a sort of external proof of organic connection (even unity) with her. In the last two groups, the motivation hinges on the question of succession to the throne; and this was exactly the question which we found lurking behind the folk-tale cycle studied in the previous chapter. The difference is that here the problem is presented from the patriarchal point of view: the king must marry to have a male heir, so that his daughter and her husband may not inherit. This new coloring is peculiar to the romances, as one might expect. In fairy tales, there is no cause for alarm when a king has daughters only. A son-in-law is considered a natural and highly desirable heir for such monarchs.

The form of the Constance-legend immortalized by Chaucer has substituted another mechanism for the opening action, as we have seen,[21] in order to reduce the heroine to her first condition of distress. A wicked mother-in-law is used in the first part as well as in the second, though she is not, of course, the same mother-in-law. A trace of a different beginning may perhaps be detected

---

[20] The Incestuous Father episode found its way into the biography of Saint Barbara, as told by Hermann von Fritslar. "Dise jungfrowe was sô schône daz ir eigin vater begerte si zu nemene zu einer êlîchen vrowen, and liz einen turn bûwen dar ûffe her si wolde behalden, und hiz zwei venster dar în machen." Das *Heili-genleben*, Leipzig, 1845, 12.

[21] For the relation of Gower and Chaucer to their source and to each other, see E. Lücke, *Das Leben der Constanze bei Trivet, Gower und Chaucer*, Anglia, XIV, 1892, 77-112 and 147-185; also the note on p. 132 ff. Cf. summary of *Man of Law's Tale*, Ch. I.

in the unwillingness of Constance to reveal herself to her father when she returns to Rome in exile. Her reticence where he is concerned is probably due to superseded versions in which she is fleeing from her father because he wanted to marry her.

Gower and Chaucer both retain from Trivet the rebuffed suitor[22] and his spectacular revenge. All three have been led by the change in the opening to a duplication of the persecution by a mother-in-law. Gower explains in one line the reason for this animosity on the part of the Soudan's mother, apart from her resentment about the change of religion. She laments the coming of a younger queen

Fore min estate shall so be lassed.

This is the universal grievance already noticed in folk-tales, still strong and remarkably potent in romance.

Other authors modify the opening situation in order to soften the effect.[23] In *Il Pecorone,* Dionigia flees from her father, not to avoid marriage with him, but to escape alliance with the aged and unattractive Signore of Alamagna, who has been chosen as

[22] See O. Siefken, *Das geduldige Weib in der englischen Lit.*, Rathenow, 1903. The author points out that this incident of the bloody dagger is an importation by Trivet or his source from the Crescentia-cycle, and should not be used, therefore, as proof of the identity of Constance and Þyrð. The use of the bloody dagger is a popular feature. It appears in *Seghelijn van Jerusalem, Tristan de Nantueil, Roman de la Violette.*

[23] It has been suggested that the Constance-story, outside of the Trivet modifications, owes something to the familiar legend of Apollonius of Tyre (cf. Suchier, Introd. lxxxv). In the latter, however, the father's desire is gratified and the princess does not escape; whereas in the Constance-group, she always avoids the marriage by flight. Each formula remains perfectly distinct in all of its versions: there is no evidence of contamination. The Greek romance may, however, form independent evidence of the father-daughter situation as survival. Erwin Rohde conjectures that the incest is a detachable part added and clumsily interwoven with the main plot to explain the wanderings of the hero afterwards. We have seen that, except in rare cases of superior plot-structure such as *Vita Offae I*, the episode is equally detachable in the Constance-saga, is used to motivate the heroine's exile, and could as easily be replaced by other formulae such as a wicked stepmother or an impious father from modern fairy tales. The importance of Apollonius as a possible influence on Constance comes from the circumstance that it was known in England at the time when the Offa-Constance story was taking shape there. The wording of the first part of the Anglo-Saxon prose Apollonius does remind one of the beginning of *La Manekine:* the death of the Queen, the growing up of the princess, and the father's failure to marry her to any one of her suitors; but the similarity, such as it is, ends there. The alleged similarity of Constance's exposure at sea and the drifting of Apollonius's wife (supposedly dead) in her coffin, seems to me fortuitous. The latter situation is used in *Jourdains de Blaivies* in a foreign context.

husband for her. In *Il Pentamerone*, an incestuous brother is substituted for the usual father from whom the heroine flees. But throughout the most of the group, as we have seen, the elements of the first adventure have remained true to form, and they present no startling deviations from the material contained in similar folktales.

This is even more definitely noticeable in the treatments of the second half of the story. The heroine has in all of them to become the consort of the king in whose lands she found refuge from her unnatural parent (or the Sultan's mother). When she is doomed to go forth once more, miserable and helpless, her persecutor is usually the old mother of her husband, and the machination against her is set in motion by the forging of an exchanged letter. The king, who has gone to war, awaits tidings of the birth of his expected child. The messenger who bears the good tidings, however, rests over night at the castle of the jealous old queen. She changes the letter to a report of the birth of animals or monsters; and, on the return of the messenger, she substitutes a command for the death of her daughter-in-law, in place of the humane reply of the king. The heroine is allowed to go into exile nevertheless; and she remains there until her husband finds her. For us, the interesting feature of this section of the story is the presence of a persecuting mother-in-law, fierce and cruel as in the folktales. Her indignation at the supposed unworthy marriage of her son causes her to retire in anger to a distant castle of her own. Yet this indignation does not seem plausible in versions where the heroine appears in radiant apparel, with a golden crown on her head.[24] In one romance only, *La Comtesse d'Anjou*, the traditional mother-in-law is replaced by the aunt of the Countess's husband. This deviation only throws into sharper relief the unanimity of the other versions.

If the heroine has not lost her hand or hands through her first misadventure, she very frequently loses them in the second, as does Hélène de Constantinople, for instance.[25] Sometimes she retains

---

[24] E.g., *Emare*, l. 349 ff.

[25] This legend has been enriched by the addition of features from the Eustachius-cycle. The children are separated from their mother by wild beasts; but they preserve the amputated arm which brings about a recognition. The story is also largely influenced by a local interest in Tours and its saint. Miss Rickert (*Mod. Phil.*, II, 374) supposes that the story

her hands throughout the story, as in the Chaucer group. In Trivet and his derivatives, many of the rudest effects are softened. The mother-in-law, Donegild, commands not the death of Constance, but her exile. She writes in her son's name that the Queen must leave the land because her presence will cause misfortune in war. Constance goes, prompted by sympathy for the folk. On her way overseas to Rome, she endures the amorous advances of a renegade heathen who joins her "en la Mere despayn envers la terre del orient." She escapes this danger, however, as she had escaped from the amorous seneschal who accused her falsely before her marriage, and finds shelter in Rome. It would seem logical for her to seek her father, since she parted from him amicably. Probably she does not because her story had been told otherwise by a predecessor of Trivet.

The most interesting feature of all is the accusation contained in the forged letters. It is quite harmonious with the folk-tale nature of the plot. The mother-in-law of La Manekine writes "monster" instead of "son"; in *La Belle Hélène*, the letter reads "deux monstres tant ydeux que apeinnes est il home qui les ose regarder"; in *Mai und Beaflor*, it reports the birth of a devil; in the Chaucer group, again, a monster; in *Il Pecorone*, "due bertuccini piu sozzi e piu contraffatti che mai si vedessero"; in *Emare*, a monster with the head of a lion, a bear, and a dragon. Thus most of the romances. Only in Fazio's chronicle and the Olive-stories is the prevailing accusation changed to one more modern and familiar to us. In the former, the Queen is accused of adultery and other nefarious acts; in the latter, the accusation of a monstrous birth is heightened by the addition "che la [Uliva] debbe esser qualche meretrice." The overwhelming majority of cases remain märchen-like in the handling of accuser and accusation.

Although many modifications have crept into this type-story from time to time, the much-used plot has remained fairly constant. The

---

took its present form at Tours, and had its origin from sources in York "in which the story of the innocent wife had come to be influenced by some legend of St. Helen, mother of Constantine, perhaps through a confusion of Tiberius Constantine with Constantine the Great." I do not think, however, that St. Helena need be invoked to explain *La Belle Hé-* *lène*. Her story, as told by Jaques d'Acqui, *Chron. Imaginis Mundi, Historiae Patriae Monumenta*, III, 1390-1392, has no resemblance, so far as I can see, to the present cycle.

The folk-books about Helena the Patient (Helena de Verduldige, in Dutch) are very close to the romance.

foregoing analysis of episodes shows clearly that the Constance-story is made up of two separable formulae, either of which may be used separately. In the Chaucer group, the persecution comes from mothers-in-law alone; in *Yde et Olive, Le Miracle, Vita Offæ I, Das Heiligenleben*,[26] and an episode of *Belle Hélène*,[26a] from fathers only. Yet, in most versions, these two figures are associated, and associated in the same manner. The persistent features are still those noticed in märchen and in popular belief: a *credible* accusation of bearing animals; jealousy on the part of a mother-in-law; exchanged letters; exposure of mother and children in the forest or at sea; the desire of a father to marry his daughter because of some mysterious factor of identity with her mother, added to a concern for the succession to the throne. The accusations are strange enough, but still, except in the isolated case of Fazio, the malevolent old queen-mother does not quite dare to accuse her daughter-in-law of the new crime of infidelity.

The motivation is equally recognizable in a second cycle of malevolent queen-mothers and persecuted queens: the story of the Swan Children. This cycle is the subject of a world of literature in itself, both critical and imaginative. It presents many problems, from totemism and metamorphosis on the one hand to the Crusades and heraldry[27] on the other. It touches problems of history[28] and of folk-tales.[29] Fortunately its significance here is definitely limited. Since the mother of the Swan Knight is a persecuted lady, we need only inquire of what she is accused and how she is restored to her former dignity, and whether her story shows traits of popular literature. A much reduced statement of the plot reveals quite as many märchen elements as those identified in the preceding cycle. A king out hunting in the forest discovers a fair and mysterious lady, no doubt a *fée*, and brings her home to marry her. His mother hates her and resents her presence. When the young queen bears seven children at once, her antagonist substitutes seven puppies and orders the infants killed. They are exposed instead, found by a hermit, and brought up by him in the forest. The old queen,

---

[26] Cf. p. 74, n.
[26a] The escape of the Princess of Bavaria from her incestuous father, MS. Bibl. Nat. 12,482, fol. 57 ff.
[27] J. F. D. Blöde, *Der historische Schwanritter*, ZfRP XXI, 1ff. and 176 ff.
[28] H. von der Hagen, *Die Schwanensage, Abhandlungen der berliner Akademie der Wissenschaften*, 1846, 564 ff.
[29] No. 49 of Grimm.

learning of their existence, sends an agent to dispose of them. He does so by removing from their necks the silver birth-chains which indicate their origin from a supernatural mother. Only one escapes. It is this child who vindicates his mother—imprisoned for many years in the palace—and restores the other children to their human form. One child alone, whose chain is destroyed, must remain a swan.

Such is the story told by Johannes de Alta Silva in his Latin *Dolopathos*,[30] a European off-shoot of the great cycle of the Seven Sages of Rome.[31] According to Johannes, the child who brings about the disenchantment of its swan-brothers and the restoration of its mother is a girl. This trait recalls the analogous tale Die sechs Schwäne of Grimm. In Johannes we have, besides, a jealous old queen of the traditional type, who achieves revenge for diminished honor by the familiar accusation. The story of Johannes has several unmistakable popular traits; and he himself reports these things "non ut visa sed ut audita."[32] The chief persecutor, the accusation of animal birth, the return of children to vindicate their mother, are all familiar elements. The antiquity of the legend and its relation to the general cycle of persecuted heroines have long been recognized.[33] The punishment of the young mother, who is buried up to her breast in the palace, is strongly suggestive of the tale of the Envious Sisters, discussed in the preceding chapter. The similarity is enhanced by the presence of the same accusation and the same solution. Huet has argued[34] that the story of the Swan Children owes much directly to the story of the Envious Sisters, which must therefore have been current in Lorraine in the twelfth century. He does not think the story became known to Europe from Eastern sources only after the Renascence; he even

---

[30] Ed. Alfons. Hilka, Heidelberg, 1913.

[31] The Swan Children story is not to be found in the Seven Sages proper. Cf. A. J. Botermans, *Die Hystorie van die seven wijse Mannen van Romen*, Harlem, 1898, 21 *et passim*; Killis Campell, *The Seven Sages of Rome*, New York, 1907, Introduction.

Johannes wrote in the last decade of the twelfth century, or thereabouts. Early in the next century a version appeared in verse by one Herbert le Clerc: *Le Roman de Dolopathos*, pub. Paris, 1856.

[32] It has been suggested that Johannes heard the tale as an orally delivered *chanson*, not as a fairy tale in our sense of the word. See Huet, *Sur quelques Formes de la Légende du Chevalier au Cygne*, Romania, XXXIX, 206-214.

[33] See von der Hagen's article, alluded to above; also G. Paris, Romania, XIX, 314-340.

[34] *De Gids*, 1906[2], 415-440.

doubts the necessity of assuming an Eastern origin. He, like Todd and Paris, admits the pertinence of Grimm's 49th tale concerning the six brothers who were bewitched into swans. There, it will be remembered, the brothers are unspelled by a sister who must weave shirts for them during seven years of silence; and her mother-in-law takes advantage of her muteness to practise the usual fraud and accuse her of bearing animals. The prominence of the sister in Johannes is therefore supposed to be a primitive trait, even though the mother, not the sister herself, is the accused queen in *Dolopathos*. The relations here are difficult to determine, beyond several points of similarity with the Envious Sisters tale. I should be tempted to say that mothers-in-law are probably older than sisters as persecutors, if we may judge from the instances reviewed; and in the Swan Children story we have a mother-in-law.[35] Let us see what becomes of her and her accusation in succeeding versions.

La Naissance du Chevalier au Cygne,[36] a poem of the twelfth century, is not directly connected with this inquiry, for a very simple reason. The young Queen here dies at the birth of her seven children, and so she is removed from the possibility of being persecuted. The change is a step towards refining the story and bringing it closer to the beliefs of a more civilized state of society. But the change does weaken the motivation for the exposure of the children. One can only assume that the King's mother is actuated by the old tribal jealousy. The seven children are born during their father's absence. The old Queen Matrosilie appears to be scandalized by the plural birth. When the maids tell her that there are seven children she replies:

 1297 VII! por la bele crois, mervelle avés contee,
   Jo ne vauroie mie qu'ele[37] me fust mostree;
   Plevissiés ça vos fois que c'ert cose celee,
   N'a home ne a feme qui de mere soit nee
   Ne sera ceste cose ja par vos revelee.

This is the nearest approach to an explanation for the command

---

[35] Huet, in *De Gids*, is one of the few to parallel the incidents of the story with popular custom and belief. He cites actual cases of belief in the birth of animals from human mothers; remarks that the Exchanged Letter device in the Constance-group is less primitive than the substitution of real animals here; and accounts for the prominence of women in such stories, from the fact that women are the chief tellers of märchen.

[36] Published by Henry Alfred Todd, *Mod. Lang. Assn. of America*, IV, 245.

[37] Sc. *la portee*.

that the children be put into baskets and disposed of by a retainer: the feeling, namely, that it is a disgrace for a woman to have borne more than one child at a time. As the *Lay of the Ash* and *Galerent* testify, this event had come to be regarded, with the growing comprehension of paternity, as a sign of infidelity on the mother's part. It is a new possibility to be reckoned with in the cycle of persecuted queens.[38] No wonder Matrosilie was horrified at the thought of seven simultaneous grandchildren!

In the so-called *Beatrix* version[39] of the Swan Children, the exposure of the infants is further prepared by a harsh trait in their mother. Before the birth of her own children, Beatrix has thrown doubt on the parenthood of a beggar woman's twins, in accordance with the superstition that such children must have two different fathers. When she herself bears six sons and a daughter, her mother-in-law Matabrune ("de plus male vielle n'oit nus hom parler") reminds her triumphantly of her own words, removes the children, and shows seven puppies to her son, King Oriant, in their place. Thus she acts the part of avenging justice, though she is still the fairy-tale persecutor as well. At the conclusion of this story, the son who vindicates his mother, the swan knight Helyas, has become so prominent that he completely overshadows his sister who, in Johannes and the Grimm fairy tale, bring about the disenchantment. A sister is still present, but she has no distinctive part, and could as well be a seventh brother. It may be noticed too that in this version, and others following it, the heinousness of the Queen's supposed offense is emphasized in a rather surprising manner. In the *Chevalier au Cygne* published by Baron Reiffenberg, Beatrix is openly accused of committing adultery with a dog, just before she is rescued by her son. This accusation, itself not without parallels in popular literature, is taken up and repeated more

---

[38] The idea may be found also among less "civilized" folk than the audiences of the Middle Ages. "Among various savages," says Edward Westermarck, "it is the custom that, if a woman gives birth to twins, one or both of them are destroyed. They are regarded sometimes as an indication of unfaithfulness on the part of the mother—in accordance with the notion that one man cannot be the father of two children at the same time —and sometimes as an evil portent or as the result of the wrath of a fetish." (*The Origin and Development of the Moral Ideas*, London, 1906, I, 395.) Cf. Kühn und Schwartz, *Norddeutsche Sagen*, 208; another version, 257; Paul the Deacon, *History of the Langobards*, I, 15; J. W. Wolf, *Ned. Sagen*, 57.

[39] Ed. C. Hippeau, Paris, 1874; also by Baron de Reiffenberg, Brussels, 1846.

or less circumstantially in the French, Flemish, and English prose redactions which followed the verse in popular favor.[40] Another interesting feature is the frequent appearance of the name Macaire for the agent and champion of Matabrune. This is a name elsewhere connected with queens unjustly accused in romances. It is associated with the more courtly, un-popular plots to be considered later, in which a villain is both accuser and persecutor, instead of a fairy-tale queen-mother. Thus, in the Swan Children cycle, very old traits exist side by side with rudimentary modern ones.

The remaining members of the family of stories require comment only for the sake of their divergences. In the *Isomberte*[41] romance, preserved only in Spanish form in chapters 47-48 of the compendious *Gran Conquista de Ultramar*, the plot has been combined ingeniously with the device of the Exchanged Letter. The old Queen is still there, with her familiar hostility; but, instead of substituting real puppies for the children, she merely writes the word in the letter originally dispatched by the faithful seneschal to her absent son. The beginning and end of the story are, however, unmistakably of the Swan Children formula.[42]

In two miracle plays, French and Italian, the plot has been notably simplified by the omission of the swan-metamorphosis. In the French play,[43] it is not clear why the old Queen hates her daughter-in-law Osanne. Nothing is said of her being found in a forest. She undergoes both forms of suffering possible for a persecuted heroine: imprisonment and exile. Her reunion with husband and sons occurs in Jerusalem.

It is perhaps little known that a version of Osanne's story is included in the unpublished *chanson de geste Theseus de Cologne* and in the prose redaction which so faithfully follows it.[44] This treatment is remarkable for a very significant change in the identity of Osanne's persecutor. Her behavior and tactics are those of the

---

[40] See Grimm's *Deutsche Sagen*, no. 534; L. Ph. C. van den Berg's *De Nederlandsche Volksromanen*, 1838.

[41] *Romania*, XIX, 320 ff.

[42] When the heroine is discovered in the forest in the beginning, she says that she has run away from her father because he wanted her to marry, in spite of her theoretical objections to marriage. Yet she has no objections to marriage with Eustache, who finds her. This illogical explanation shows clearly the influence of stories in which she had run away to avoid marriage with her own father.

[43] L. J. N. Monmerqué and Francisque Michel, *Théâtre Français du Moyen-Age*, Paris, 1839, 551.

[44] For a summary of this section of the romance, see Appendix II, no. 2.

usual mother-in-law, but she herself, Clodas, is an ambitious lady of the court, widow of one of the King's late enemies, who is anxious to rehabilitate her fortunes by marrying the King. To do this, she must rid herself of the Queen. Hence the accusation of animal birth, the substitution of puppies, the exposure of the three children.[45] When these sons are grown, Clodas identifies them and continues to fight against them, but she loses in the end. She is, throughout, a scheming woman with political ambitions. In comparison with Matabrune, she is a very Elizabethan figure. Her desires are clear and un-witchlike, but her methods belong to fairy tales still: the old accusation of an animal parturition, and the exposure of the children. Because Clodas represents a development away from fairy tales—a change observable in other medieval romances—she has an important place in the gallery of accusers. And the romance, *Theseus de Cologne,* in which she does her mischief, is a highly diverting tale, well worth rescuing from the obscurity in which it at present reposes.

The Italian play of *Stella* belongs more particularly to the Exchanged Letter class,[46] but the name of its heroine, Stella, seems to be taken from the Italian poem on the Swan Children: *Istoria della Regina Stella e Mattabruna.* The play is compounded of several motives. Here a wicked stepmother acts as double persecutor. She first drives the girl from her home, and later changes the second letter to a command for Stella's execution.

>Considerando como d'adulterio
>Ha fatto duo figlino' la fraudolente.[47]

The accusation shows a certain relation to the belief underlying some of the later forms of the Swan Children tale: the impossibility for one father to have more than one child at a time. Through quite natural transitions, this becomes an unqualified accusation of infidelity; but only after the transitions as we have noticed them: (1) accusation of the birth of animals; (2) accusation of the birth of animals and of infidelity because of the plurality of offspring; (3) accusation of infidelity pure and simple.

---

[45] *Theseus* resembles the miracle play in the reduction of the number of children to three.

[46] *Sacre Rappresentazioni dei Secoli XIV, XV, XVI,* Florence, 1872.
[47] *Ibid.,* 317.

It would be easy to extend the versions indefinitely, by including the endless prose books on the Knight of the Swan, in many languages. The story, having been current in the Low Countries in verse based on the French, appeared in prose soon after the invention of printing. The oldest Flemish prose version appeared in Antwerp early in the sixteenth century; and although the oldest extant copy from Holland proper is supposedly one from Amsterdam in 1651,[48] we know that others must have existed before it.[49] The edition of 1763, for instance, has its license (*approbatie*) dated from 1547. The tale was reprinted again and again, with very slight changes in wording and spelling, through the eighteenth and nineteenth centuries. In France, the story appeared in print as early as 1504; Copland's translation into English was set up in the type of Wynkyn de Worde in 1512. These popular books contribute nothing new to our knowledge of the story. Their virtue consists in their quaint woodcuts, their earnestness of style, and (especially in the Dutch) their delightful vigor of phraseology. They also indicate the great popularity of the theme long after the passing of the Middle Ages. In English, it is true, the story did not enjoy a long career of popularity and reprintings, as it did in Dutch. But it was familiar enough to readers in the sixteenth century on both sides of the Channel.

Considered as a whole, the series of stories included in the Swan Children cycle has a distinct bearing on the general problem of persecuted queens in literature. It is another example, like the Constance-story, of a very primitive accusation adopted in medieval literature and retained there with a fair degree of clarity. There is, to be sure, a tendency to develop the märchen accuser into a more literary type (Clodas); and the accusation undergoes several changes, as we have seen, until it emerges at times as the more modern charge of infidelity pure and simple. In this, it differs from the accusation in the Exchanged Letter group. There the plot, also composed of märchen elements, remained more rigidly constant; and the tendency to substitute a reasonable and credible

---

[48] W. Nijhoff, *Catalogus van Boeken*, Pt. V, col. 180 ff. But there is a copy in the Leiden University Library from Amsterdam which is catalogued as ca. 1543.

[49] Cf. W. de Vreese, *Tijdschrift voor Ned. Taal- en Letterkunde*, 1894, 38-52. Copies of the 1651 edition are in Leiden and The Hague.

accusation for the obsolescent primitive one, appears only in two minor instances. Here, on the other hand, a logical evolution of the original primitive accusation is evident, even while the accuser remains generally the same person: a begrudging mother-in-law, whose prominence is unquestioned in both cycles. In these groups, therefore, characters and plots have generally remained true to märchen formulae, with no accusation of infidelity and no villain or spurned lover as accuser. In the next group we shall find the malicious mother-in-law threatened by the introduction of a new, subsidiary character.

CHAPTER IV

THE ACCUSED QUEEN IN ROMANCE *cont'd*: THE ADVENT OF THE VILLAIN

THE mother-in-law holds sway in other romances than those examined in the preceding chapter, but in them her preëminence is not unchallenged. She appears as a person of fading rank and significance, literally speaking, in the cycles of Octavian and Valentine. The active execution of the villainy is taken over more and more by a courtier-aide, who becomes the favored character of the future. In the Octavian stories, the process can be observed clearly. The accusation develops, too, as did Matabrune's, into a charge of infidelity pure and simple.

The legend of the Emperor Octavian[1] probably goes back to a *chanson de geste* of the twelfth century[2] which had a plot much like that of the romance *Octavian*. A much longer, more cluttered romance called *Florent et Octavian* dates from the fourteenth century. It has a similar beginning, but the latter part of the story is burdened with many duplicated and imported adventures which appear to be secondary parasitic growths. It shows advantageously the change from fairy-tale motivation which one would expect in a fourteenth-century romance. From the earlier form, *Octavian*, or from an almost identical version, are derived two Middle English metrical romances; from *Florent et Octavian*, chapters 42-52 of Book II of *Reali di Francia*, and the folk-books.

The earlier romance tells the tale of a mother-in-law who is very angry—without reason, it would appear at first—at the birth of two

---

[1] The versions discussed here are:
Octavian, ed. Karl Vollmöller, Heilbronn, 1883.
Octavian (two Middle English versions), ed. Gregor Sarrazin, Heilbronn, 1885.
Florent et Octavian, MS. in Bibl. Nat., summary in *Hist. Lit.*, XXVI, 303 ff.
I Reali di Francia, ed. Giuseppi Vandelli, Bologne, 1892.

Folk Books: See P. O. Bäckström, *Svenska Folkböcker*, I, 235-236, and Paul Streve, *Die Octavian Sage*, Erlangen, 1884. The story was evidently popular in its prose dress. It was published as *Florent et Lyon*, Troyes, 1534; and as the *Histori von dem Keyser Octaviano und seinem Weib und zweyen Sünen*, Strassburg, 1535.
[2] Vollmöller's introduction, xviii.

grandchildren. She accuses the Queen of unfaithfulness, and bribes a youth to lie beside her in Octavian's place while the young mother is asleep. Octavian, convinced by the sight, kills the youth and sends his wife and children into exile. The two boys are carried off by kidnapping beasts in a forest, but the mother soon recovers one of them and continues her journey into the Orient, accompanied by a kindly lion. Years later, the family is reunited by a war with the Saracens around Paris. Octavian and his sons come there to help King Dagobert, and finally recognize one another. Octavian has already discovered the fraud of his mother, and so he takes back his wife, who has persisted, in spite of everything, in an attitude of invincible humility.

Here we have the accusation of infidelity based, as in the Swan Children cycle, on the birth of more than one child; but this ancient charge is further supported by ocular evidence for the benefit of the Emperor Octavian. Step by step, we are finding the old explanations and accusations supplanted by new ones. For the first time, a definite person is employed to bear the blame of being the Queen's lover.

The two Middle English versions—derived separately in Northern and Southern England from the French original—do not present any striking peculiarities, except in vividness of style and striking picturesque effects, especially in the scenes where the innocence of the wronged Queen is contrasted with the dastardly behavior of the mother-in-law.[3] The same folk-tale King's mother is to be found in *Florent et Octavian*.

The Empress Florimonde bears twins in her husband's absence. When Octavian returns home, his mother meets him and accuses Florimonde of licentious behavior. She urges him to disown the children. But he will not do so when he sees that each of them has a red-cross birthmark. So the old woman bribes a page to become her tool. Florimonde and her two sons are exiled; and the major part of the romance concerns the adventures and exploits of this exile. During a war with the Saracens the senior Octavian is captured, and his wicked mother is left to rule the besieged city of Rome. The younger Octavian fights in defence of the city; but he openly accuses his grandmother and, like Helyas, defeats her champion. In the midst of episodes amorous and military, he rescues his father and his brother Florent from the heathen, and brings about the reconciliation between his mother and father.

[3] When the Emperor and his mother break into the room he smites off the head of the rash youth

. . . and also warm
He ðrew þat hedde with lowryng chere
Into þe lady barm.
(Southern *Oct.* l. 208.)

88   CHAUCER'S CONSTANCE AND ACCUSED QUEENS

I Reali di Francia has a peculiar interest. Just as the story of the Swan Children's mother was modified to make her sufferings consonant with poetic justice, so the woes of Drusolina, here, are rendered more endurable for a reader because they are due to overweening pride. Perhaps, indeed, the incident is a direct borrowing from the Matabrune group.

The story relates how a poor woman comes to the court of young King Fioravante to beg for help, since her warrior husband is dead and she is unable to support her twin children. Drusolina says haughtily, "It cannot be that two children were born of one father at one time." Fioravante interposes, "Do not say that, Drusolina, because nothing is impossible to God," and he gives gold to the woman. Later Drusolina herself becomes the mother of twins. While she is asleep, the King's mother bids Antonio, a young cupbearer, stay beside her, everyone else being out of the room, "for a jest." He protests that this would be unfitting, but she insists. Then she hurries to Fioravante and slanders the two, saying that the children must be Antonio's. The King rushes in and kills Antonio; the Queen is finally allowed to go into exile instead of being burnt. Her adventures and her sons' are like those of Florimonde and her children. In the end, it is the kindly lion who restores the members of the family to one another, and gives Fioravante the opportunity to ask pardon of Drusolina for his too great credulity years before. And the grandmother is burned, to the profound satisfaction of all concerned.[4]

The group about Octavian's mother is another evidence, like the *Man of Law's Tale*, of the vitality of that malicious power attributed, in folk-tales, to royal mothers-in-law. These stories show her still in the full exercise of that power, but new motives and accusations are beginning to spring up around her: the accusation of illegitimacy of the children is used in place of the substitution of animals; the old stigma attached to the birth of more than one child at once is brought up again; the old queen's tool, the guileless if stupid courtier, complicates the action by the addi-

---

[4] The folk-books offer little subject for comment. The Swedish may be taken as typical. When Octavian's wife bears twins, his mother plots evil against her. First, she slanders the Queen to her son, saying "that the two children were not his." When he refuses to listen, she persuades an underling that the King would like to be rid of his wife, and would appreciate as well as reward a pretext for putting her away. Of course the Emperor kills the misguided courtier and casts his wife and children into prison to await the stake. The Queen protests her innocence and begs for mercy in behalf of the children. He finally grants her exile instead of death. The rest of the story follows the usual lines.

tion of a supposed lover. In the presence of these new, or at least additional factors, the hostility of the old queen is allowed to pass unexplained more often than not; and her traditional jealousy seems to be more than ever a heritage from forgotten times. It does not fit well with accusations of infidelity, which are becoming increasingly popular.

Another group of stories centers about the figure of a persecuting mother-in-law: the family of legends which are to be traced to a French original (now lost) concerning two heroes, Valentine and Nameless—probably Sansnom in the French.[5] The most vehement persecuting is still done by the king's mother, but beside her stands another figure of increasing importance: a wicked villain who has determined on the destruction of the queen for reasons of his own. In the Valentine-tales, the motives of this evil creature are not made clear. He is therefore a needless duplication of the fairy-tale persecutor, and his presence seems to indicate a transition.

In the evolution of the story, there are two phases to be distinguished, just as in the Octavian group. Again, the earlier form is simpler, while the later is burdened with bewildering adventures. The former goes by the name of *Valentine and Nameless;* the latter is called *Valentine and Oursson* from the existent French (and other) folk-books. The Middle Dutch[6] poem which is derived from the older French form is unfortunately too fragmentary to reveal clearly the story in its complete form, but this lack is supplied by a Middle Low German poem[7] which gives the entire narrative. Whether the Dutch is dependent on the Low German or vice versa[8] makes little difference here, since the story was in any case widely known. Thus it is told in the poem called *Valentines Bôk:*

King Pippin has a sister Phila and a daughter Clarina. King Crisostomus of Hungary asks for the hand of the fair Phila in marriage, and word is sent back to Hungary that his request is granted. He rejoices, but his mother is wroth.

---

[5] The Dutch version from which we deduce the hypothetical French ancestor has the form Nameloos.

[6] G. Kalff, *Middelnederlandsche epische Fragmenten,* Groningen, 1885, no. xi.

[7] W. Seelmann, *Valentin und Namelos,* Leipzig, 1884.

[8] Kalff (208) holds the former view; Seelmann thinks the German the older form.

> 43 Crisostomus wart der mere vro
> unde al sîn gesinde dô,
> sunder siner moder was dat leit.

Crisostomus decides to ride to Pippin's court to receive his bride, and invites his court to accompany him. His mother and her confederate, Bishop Frankhart, refuse. The King thereupon expresses extreme anger, and Bishop Frankhart retracts. But the two evil ones nourish their resentment; and, when the marriage is celebrated at Pippin's court, they await their opportunity. An astrologer announces that Phila is to become the mother of twins. The Bishop and the old Queen arrange to drown the children at birth. Their ferocity is quite unaccounted for. The maid to whom the task is entrusted exposes one of the boys in the forest, where a wolf adopts him; and she sets the other afloat in a box carefully provided with air holes.

Phila's husband asks her where her children are. She does not know. His mother "bets" (ik weddes!) that Phila has murdered them, and Crisostomus believes this primitive accusation. Even Pippin, Phila's brother, yields full belief from the beginning. When she is tried,

> 269 do sprak ere broder 'du dumme wîf,
> wes nemestu den kinderen ere lif?'

The bishop makes a speech in which he asserts that she has confessed her guilt. She pulls his hair, denying it fiercely. Pippin insists that she should be burnt, but she is allowed to go into exile with a young knight Blandemer. She finds refuge in the castle of a maiden whom they meet and rescue on the way.

Meantime one of the children, Valentine, has been found drifting on the water by Clarina, his cousin. When he is grown up he encounters his savage brother in the forest and tames him. There follow various adventures for Valentine and Nameless which do not affect the fundamental plot. Their mother has yet to be reunited to them. In her castle asylum, she has been forced to repulse the love of a wicked knight Gawin, who thereupon murders the young princess with whom she is sleeping, and hurries to awaken the King. Phila of course protests her innocence and horror at the deed. She is to be burnt nevertheless; but at the last moment her two sons come riding up with Blandemer. Valentine fights for her and rescues her, not knowing who she is. He leaves her with a regret he cannot understand, and proceeds on his quest to find his parents. There is dramatic irony in their situation, which is repeated when the two brothers help their own father, again unwittingly. Next day they encounter a serpent which addresses them with the unexpected remark: "Follow me and learn about your parents." It leads them to the castle of a maiden from whom they learn what they wish to know; Phila is rescued by her son from a second predicament; the family is reunited; and the Bishop is punished.

THE ACCUSED QUEEN IN ROMANCE 91

The enveloping story of Phila, aside from the numerous chivalric adventures which fill her exile and her children's, is clearly composed of standard märchen ingredients: wicked mother-in-law (as in the Constance-story, and the Swan Children and Octavian cycles), credulous king, accusation of child-murder (as in *Esmoreit*), and exposure of children. When the unnecessary Bishop is removed, the folk-tale constitution of the framing plot becomes more apparent. Let the Queen stay in prison instead of going into exile, and the similarity is even more striking. The enveloping plot belongs to märchen; the discursive central action is medieval romance pure and simple. The relation of the parts is the same in all other treatments of Valentine and Nameless. The German[9] and Swedish[10] prose versions are very similar in plot and wording. Again the Bishop and the mother-in-law conspire, and again Phila's credulous fairy-tale husband and her brother believe the inhuman fairy-tale accusation of child-murder. Surely the story can not be considered quite apart from the logic of folk-lore and popular literature if one is to understand the behavior of the chief characters in the opening action.[11]

We meet one of these persecutors again in *Valentine and Ourson*,[12] the elaborated form of the fiction in French prose, and in the many folk-books descended from it. Here the nature of the motives becomes clearer. Whereas in *Valentine and Nameless* no reason was given for the animosity of the Bishop, in *Valentine and Oursson* the Bishop's persecution is motivated, and motivated in a very significant fashion. The primitive mother-in-law is suppressed entirely, and he commits the villainy alone—all because of

---

[9] Seelmann, 74-104.
[10] G. E. Klemming, *Namnlös och Valentin, en Medeltids-Roman*, Stockholm, 1846.
[11] For fragments of other versions see *Altdeutsche Blätter*, Leipzig, 1836, I, 204-206; Kalff, *Epische Fragmenten*, no. xi; Seelmann, Introduction; Klemming, Introduction.
In the latter part of the Dutch folk-book *Malegijs*, a similar archaic charge is brought against a young Queen for equally archaic reasons. The King of Armenia has married a maiden beneath his class, who is hated by her mother-in-law. The old lady therefore sets her grandchild adrift and accuses the Queen of killing her own child. The arrival of a kindly *fée*, Oriande, resolves the trouble without any fatalities; but the situation must have been familiar enough to readers in the Low Countries even before the publication of *Malegijs*. The use of such an accusation, here as in *Valentine and Nameless* and in *Esmoreit*, is surely a survival.
[12] A study of the sources of this romance is being prepared by Mr. Arthur Dickson, of Columbia University.

the pangs of unrequited love. These changes constitute an approach to the realm of courtly love and courtly literature, far away from fairy tales and their ogreish characters. The discomfited ecclesiastic reports to Bellisant's husband that she has confessed the sin of infidelity to him. The credulous monarch sends her into exile with one companion, who is very soon forced to protect her from the pursuing Archbishop, in sight of a witness. The Queen bears her children alone in the forest. One of them—Oursson, of course —is carried off by a bear, and the other is taken by Pippin while she is lying unconscious. Meantime the villain accuser has been challenged and defeated by the merchant who witnessed his pursuit of the Queen. Thus the truth about the accusation has been brought to light, but the story is not near its conclusion. When the younger generation, Valentine and his bearish brother, become the center of attention, they are involved in a long series of fantastic adventures which have no pertinence to the skeleton plot. Valentine appears several times as the rescuer of his father; but, in the end, he kills him unwittingly in a battle against the heathen in Hungary. He retires from the world to do seven years' penance for learning and practising the black art.[18]

In spite of a general resemblance to the earlier *Valentine and Nameless*, the prose romance has clearly been transformed by the presence of many new elements. Either these additional elements existed in the common French source of *Valentine and Nameless* and *Valentine and Oursson*, and were suppressed in *Valentine and Nameless;* or, *Valentine and Oursson* has made additions which required essential changes as well. Probably the latter is the case here, as with *Octavian* and its later modification *Florent and Octavian*. The changes in both pairs of romances are instructively

---

[18] The remarks on *Valentine and Oursson* are based on the Paris edition of 1525 and the Amsterdam edition of 1798 (both in the Staatsbibliothek, Munich), and those of Deventer, 1791, and Ghent (n.d.) in the British Museum. A quaint edition in German, from the British Museum, is thus entitled: In disem bůch werden begriffen und gefunden zwo wunderbarlicher hystorien ganz lieblich ze lesen/ ouch dienen ze fil erfarnyss. Die erst hystori von zweyen trüwen gesellen . . . Olivier eynes künigs sun von Algabria . . . Die ander hystori sagt von zweyen brederen Valentino und Orso/ deren vatter eyn keiser zů Constantinopel/ und ir mutter eines künigs dochter in Frankrich gewesen/ mit namen Peppin/ gezogen vss frantzosischer Zungen in dütsch durch Wilhelm Ziely von Bern in ochtlandt. Anno MDXXI.

The first story, Olivier and Artus, belongs to the Amis and Amiles type.

similar: an effacing of the mother-in-law, a change of accusation, a shift of interest from the parents to the exiled children, besides a formidable increase in the number of irresponsible, irrelevant adventures. Other medieval romances,[14] in being changed into prose folk-books, are known to have suffered the same unmerciful stretching and padding and modification of plot. Some of the transforming ingredients can be detected and separated without difficulty, especially those that affect the enveloping plot about the persecuted queen:

1. The complete disappearance of the primitive mother-in-law, and her replacement by a wicked lover, are due to the influence of stories like *Macaire*, whose name, it will be remembered, was encountered in a developed form of the Swan Children story. Macaire (see p. 104 ff.) may be taken as a type of the very wicked man, usually of Ganelon's race and character, who tries to ruin an innocent heroine because his love has been scorned. He belongs distinctly to the *chansons de geste* rather than the romances based on folk-lore. He is to be found in more than one legend concerning virtuous ladies in distress.

2. Since the mother-in-law and her gruesome accusations— which must necessarily follow the birth of children—have been disposed of, the way is left clear for a favorite and frequently recurring scene: the birth of children in a forest, far away from help. Moreover, the defeat of the villain and the vindication of the Queen are now accomplished by a champion other than a son of the Queen.

3. The chivalric additions come from a later age of story-telling than those that they supplant; primitive motives have been modified and withdrawn in favor of more modern, comprehensible ones. It has been suggested that *Valentine and Oursson* owes a direct debt to the folk-book *Octavian*. But, as Seelmann remarks,[15] all the similar traits of *Octavian* existed already in the earlier form of this story, and inferentially, in the ultimate French original of *Valentine and Nameless*. None of the special peculiarities of Octavian are to be found here. These considerations lead Seelmann to conclude "that an ancient popular märchen lurks here

---

[14] Compare, for example, the Dutch folk-book *Malegijs* with the poem *Maugis d'Aigremont*.
[15] *Op. cit.*, li-lvi.

[in the older Valentine material], which was expanded and transformed by a North French minstrel." The northern provenance of *Valentine and Oursson* seems the more probable in view of the northward spread of both *Valentine and Nameless* and *Valentine and Oursson* in the Low German dialects.[16] In the fairy tale, the bearish character of one of the brothers may well have formed a chief attraction, as indeed it still forms a marked characteristic of this family of romances.[17]

The villain male persecutor,[18] who has hovered for some time in the background, now steps forward to occupy a position of central interest. In *Le Chevalier au Cygne*, he played a minor part as Queen Matabrune's agent, who was defeated in combat by Helyas; in *Octavian*, the old Queen's agent was stupid rather than villainous; in *Valentine and Nameless*, he worked with the old Queen and served her purpose without any tangible reason, merely as a duplication of her more efficient self; and, in *Valentine and Oursson*, he has appeared at last alone, a vindictive seeker of satisfaction for spurned love. In this last romantic guise he will be seen in the next group.

---

[16] The Scandinavian recensions seem to be based on the Dutch. The British Museum, for instance, contains an Icelandic MS. (Add. 4863, fol. 229-335) of *Falentins og Ursins Saga* in which Dutch origin is indicated by the proper names: Só er skrifad í fornum sogum ad sá háborni konungr Pippin hafi first byriad sina rykesstiorn í Brabant vid Holland, Anno Christi DCXV.—Seelmann mentions a MS. in Stockholm: Eyn fogur og Fridanleg Historia . . . Furst Samsett I Fronsku Tale: Sydan aa Hollendsku.

[17] The fact that Valentine kills his long-sought father unwittingly is a commonplace of medieval romance and of popular literature generally, which may be attached to any hero who, for any reason, is early separated from his parents. It seems to be a wilful variation in *Valentine and Oursson*; since the hero has encountered his father several times before, and the time for a recognition scene, whether tragic or otherwise, is long past.

[18] In the story of Pwyll, Son of Dyved, in the *Mabinogion*, a Queen's infant son disappears in the night, and the negligent watchers smear blood on her mouth to prove that she ate him. This is an unusual transfer of the mother-in-law's accusation to minor characters. The story seems to be mutilated or incomplete in comparison with other tales of accused queens.

CHAPTER V

THE ACCUSED QUEEN IN ROMANCE *cont'd:* THE VILLAIN AS SOLE ACCUSER

A. THE AMBITIOUS ACCUSER

IN a large number of romances of the Middle Ages, the accusation of an innocent queen comes from one whose motives are quite different from those of fairy-tale persecutors: namely, rejected love or political ambition. As might be expected, this villain flourishes best in the atmosphere of the *chansons de geste,* with their feudal and patriarchal society. Treason against an innocent queen is thus brought into relation with the great tragic treason of the whole Charlemagne-cycle. Accordingly, the villain is usually made a member of the prolific race of Ganelon. Perhaps, indeed, the change from more primitive persecutors was hastened by the popularity of the *chansons de geste* and their mode of narrative. Perhaps villain-accusers of innocent queens are due entirely to the *chansons de geste.* Some of the plots would make one think so.

In harmony with these changes is the great popularity of an accusation of infidelity. The fairy-tale charges are forgotten or ignored in the new setting. The society which makes that setting is society as we know it; and the number of accusations possible is, for that very reason, narrowed down to infidelity and treason.

The stories related to *Doon de la Roche,* contained in a manuscript in the British Museum, illustrate these transformations clearly. The French *chanson de geste*[1] and the Icelandic[2] and Spanish[3]

---

[1] Brit. Mus. MS. Harl. 4404, fol. 1 ff. Published by the Soc. des An. Textes Fr. See Appendix II, no. 3.

[2] *Landres-þattr,* a retelling of a French original in the second recension of the Icelandic Karlamagnussaga. See C. R. Unger, *Karlamagnus Saga ok Kappa Hans,* Christiania, 1860, 50-75. For summaries and discussion, see appendix and Grundtvig's *Danemarks Gamle Folksviser,* Copenhagen, 1853, I, 177 ff.; F. Wolf, *Über die Oliva-Sage, Denkschriften der kaiserlichen Akademie der Wissenschaften,* Vienna, 1857, 180-282, Anhang A (Philosophisch-historische Classe).

[3] *Enrrique Fi de Oliva,* a Spanish romance also derived from the French. See F. Wolf, *Über die neuesten Leistungen der Franzosen für die Herausgabe ihrer National-Heldengedichte,* Vienna, 1833, 98-123.

recensions have a villain related explicitly to Ganelon, who is actuated by ambition, and who uses a charge of infidelity as his weapon. In the French version, this individual, Tomile by name, is a nephew of Ganelon, who slanders the heroine to Doon without any apparent reason. His method is that of Octavian's old mother: the introduction of a page into Olive's room while she lies in a drugged sleep. From the first, Doon believes in his wife's guilt, and becomes the unresisting victim of Tomile's machinations. He obediently marries Tomile's daughter, disowns his son as a bastard, and sends him into exile. It is this son, Landri, who reëstablishes his mother after adventures which, like Esmoreit's, include a love-affair with a princess in the Orient. Tomile and his daughter are confounded; and Doon and Olive are remarried, to the great satisfaction of their son.

The motivation of this narrative is not clear. One wonders why Tomile should display such animosity against Olive. His device to implicate her is conventional enough, but only later is his reason indicated: a desire to put forward his own daughter. The Spanish romance explains his behavior more definitely, through ambition alone. Here Tomillas, the father of Ganelon, exercises an undue influence on Duke de la Ronche from the beginning. He is disappointed by the Duke's marriage to Oliva, because he had wanted his sister to become Duchess. So much being clear, the rest of the action becomes easily comprehensible. Tomillas employs more complicated magical devices to produce the scene[4] which incriminates Oliva, but the scene itself, the accusation, and Oliva's protestation of innocence, are the same. Enrrique, the exiled son, also brings about the reinstatement of his mother, though not without delays and interruptions in the execution of his filial duty. The skeleton of the story and the type of its characters still correspond closely to the type set by *Esmoreit*. We have the ambitious villain as accuser, the credulous king, the son whose youth is spent in exile, and even the love-affair with a princess in foreign parts, before the vindication. Many other plots belonging to kindred cycles show a general similarity to the Dutch play.

So far, however, the accusation has not been spoken by a scorned

---

[4] Here, as in the Danish ballads to be mentioned later, she offers to undergo various tests to prove her innocence. Her offers are rejected.

lover. It has been the result of ambition rather than of hurt feelings. In the Icelandic recension, two new elements are introduced which greatly modify the situation. The persecutor, Milon, is one of the long series of wicked seneschals so popular in medieval fiction; and his attitude toward Olif is at first amorous. Having been left in charge of her during her husband's absence, he pays court to her (by solemnly comparing his age and qualities to her husband's), is properly rejected, and ruins her by a scene staged for her husband. The second new element appears immediately after this public accusation. When the Queen has vainly offered to undergo tests of innocence, a knight named Engilbert of Dynhart steps forward, strikes the villain, challenges him as a liar, and defeats him in combat. This innovation almost brings about a premature conclusion to the tale; and this conclusion would transfer to a knightly champion the office usually reserved for the Queen's son. But Milon loudly exclaims that his defeat is due to the Queen's witchcraft. She is confined in a stone tower for many years until her grown son Landri, her traditional and more successful champion, finds her and frees her. The scene resembles the end of *Esmoreit* more closely than did the corresponding one in the Spanish romance. In the earlier part of the Icelandic tale, the change from the ambitious Tomile to the false seneschal Milon has made a number of differences in the plot. The former was probably the original accuser, and his ambition was the original motive. One effect of the suppressed motivation is the unexplained marriage of the husband of Olif to Milon's daughter after the imprisonment of the first wife. This episode has become unnecessary, since the ambitious impulse of Milon has been changed to an erotic one. Grundtvig's assertion that the Icelandic is older than the Spanish version must therefore not be taken to mean that it is the more primitive in form. It does preserve a story very similar to the French and the Spanish, and all traits common to it and to the Spanish may well be assumed to be inherited from the same source; but its structure has been organically affected by a different type of plot. One person, Engilbert of Dynhart, the Queen's champion, is entirely due to this extraneous plot. He is the knight who offered to defend his lady against her accuser when all her other friends had deserted her. If he had been allowed to champion her successfully, the presence of her son would have been superfluous. So his championship remains ineffective; but the solution which he might have afforded is fully accepted in another type of stories.

B. The Seneschal as Accuser

I refer to a family of tales standing somewhat aside from these, in which the accused queen is not defended or restored by a child, but by a chivalrous and disinterested champion. In its simplest form the legend became attached to Charlemagne. It is to be found in the *Karlmeinet*,[5] developed romantically and without any indication of an historical genesis. High treason is at work as usual; treason against the knight-champion, however, rather than Queen Galia. It is because some courtiers are jealous of the noble knight Morand that they accuse him and Galia to the Emperor. Morand fights a long battle in self-defense and wins. Being accused himself, he is compelled to undertake the combat. Elsewhere, however, the champion is usually disinterested. Such tales contain a rebuffed lover as well as an innocent queen, a credulous king, and the generous champion. A group of Danish ballads edited by Grundtvig tells this type of story dramatically. These ballads generally localize the action about the city of Spires. The heroine Gunild is left in the care of a villain during her husband's absence, as in the *Landres-þattr*. She is obliged to refuse him her love (in one group, her sword), and he accuses her to her husband of infidelity—generally with an Archbishop. Bareheaded and barefoot, as in the *Landres-þattr* again, she asks for a champion in the hall, but none responds except Memering, her faithful knight. In all ballads the Queen's champion wins, and her husband begs her forgiveness. Obviously this is a new conclusion. With the imprisonment and the child removed, the central fact becomes the combat fought by one outside of the family; and that, as Gaston Paris has pointed out, is distinctly medieval.[6] There is little folklore to be detected in the story. Chivalrous institutions condition it entirely. The same essentially chivalrous plot is preserved in the

---

[5] Ed. Adelbert von Keller, Stuttgart, 1858. Galia's story is on pp. 326-431. The poem is dated by Lachmann (*ibid.*, 834) 1190-1210.

[6] *Annales du Midi*, XII, Toulouse, 1900, 26-32.

German folk-book *Ritter Galmy*,[7] the French *Palanus*,[8] and Danish *Den Kydske Dronning*,[9] in the cycle of the *Erl of Toulouse*,[10] in the Latin epistle of Jacob Wimfeling which contains a version of the Accused Queen and Wicked Seneschal formula[11] current in the fifteenth century in the region of Spires; the group of Danish and Icelandic ballads, which also localize the action in the city of Spires; and the legends told of several historical personages by medieval chroniclers.[12]

At least one simple inference may be drawn from this far-branching story. Originating as it evidently does in comparatively recent times, in centuries which saw the growth of feudalism— for the combat is the most constant feature—certainly far enough

---

[7] Simrock, *Die deutschen Volksbücher*, XI, 447 ff. The false seneschal accuses the Queen of infidelity with a cook (as in *Octavian*); Galmy disguises as a monk, hears her confession, and vindicates her innocence.

[8] Ed. from MS. by A. de Terrebasse, Lyon, 1833.

[9] C. J. Brandt, *Romantisk Digting fra Middelalderen*, Copenhagen, 1870, II, 89-128.

[10] The English romance and a number of similar Spanish ones warrant the assumption of a lost French original. The English has been edited by Gustav Lüdtke, Berlin, 1881, with a detailed account of all versions, and of possible historical bases. Two knights attempt in turn to gain the love of the Empress, and are rejected in turn. They then trick a knight into acting the part of a lover of the Empress, and stab him in the midst of the prepared scene. The Earl of Toulouse, her generous and devoted champion, convinces himself of her innocence as did Galmy, and wins the combat for her. The two villains are put to death by fire.

The Spanish versions are less complete. The motivation is not made clear. Lüdtke sees in Judith, wife of Louis the Pious, and Bernard I, Count of Barcelona and Toulouse, the historical prototypes of the Empress and her champion. He believes that the Spanish versions were brought into being by an oral Aquitanian legend concerning Bernardus "comes Tolosanus." I confess that I do not see much similarity between the political intrigues of Judith and her favorites, and the English and Spanish romances as we have them. Even if historical events furnished the kernel of these stories, romantic ingredients have completely transformed them.

Two Provençal chronicles, like the English romance, account for the accusation by means of the wicked seneschal formula (spurned love). Caesar de Nostradamus tells the story of Henry V of Germany and his Empress Mathilde; *La Royalle Couronne des Roys d'Arles* (Avignon, 1641) calls the Emperor Henry III. The rescuer is Raymond of Provence.

[11] MS. Brit. Mus., Add. 27,569, fol. 15b-21a, published in *Zeitschrift für vergleichende Litteraturgeschichte*, IV, 342-355, 1891. Jacob heard the legend in 1470 when he was journeying from Spires towards Strassbourg. The text relates how Lampertus, Duke of Burgundy, left his government and his wife in charge of Count Philopertus during his absence at war; how the Count, victim of a hopeless passion for the Duchess Eugenia, retired secretly from court; how his successor, likewise rebuked by Eugenia, accused her of adultery with the cook; how she was condemned to death because no one would fight for her; and how Philopertus returned from his self-imposed exile to champion her and kill her false accuser. The mention of a cook recalls the analogous tales of *Octavian*, *Ritter Galmy*, and *Genevieve of Brabant*.

[12] Cf., for example, Paul the Deacon's *History of the Langobards*, IV, 47.

removed from the ancient legendary state of matriarchy, it might be expected to ignore all possible accusations except the one we have found most closely associated with patriarchy; and it does. In none of these ballads or poems or chronicles for which an historical basis may for any reason be claimed, is there any charge other than infidelity. The two motives used, political ambition and spurned love, seem equally modern when set beside the jealousy of mothers-in-law. The villainy of a male persecutor is developed by distinctly modern motivation throughout.

An exception to this may be found in the thirteenth-century poem *Wolfdietrich*,[13] which is closer than the champion-stories to the general literary type because its heroine, like Chaucer's Constance and most of the others, has a child. As in *Esmoreit*, the child is the important factor in reëstablishing his mother. There is another false seneschal in *Wolfdietrich*, who is repulsed by the Queen during her husband's absence. His revenge takes the form of an intensified accusation: not only is she unfaithful, but her child is of Satanic origin. After this affair has been cleared up by the faithful Berchtung, and King Hugdietrich has died, the widowed Queen is nevertheless idiotic enough to marry the villain who has caused her so much woe,[14] in spite of all advice and her knowledge of his character. The story is, as a whole, unsatisfactorily built. The tactics of the villain after he has been repulsed, leave room for possible explanations between the virtuous Queen and her husband which would have destroyed him utterly. And the accusation is unsupported by any attempt at proof. Mothers-in-law managed things better! Perhaps the second marriage of Wolfdietrich's mother constitutes a deliberate, not very happy modification of the faithless-seneschal motif in order to connect this version of Wolfdietrich's youth with other well-known material about him and a stepfather.[15]

Wolfdietrich is probably Frankish in origin. The name of the hero's father, Hugdietrich, means Dietrich the Frank; the Franks receive the place of honor in the tale; and above all, a resemblance has been noticed between it and the French *chanson de geste*, *Parise*

---

[13] *Wolfdietrich A*: see *Das deutsche Heldenbuch*, 25-37.
[14] She is not alone in doing this. Countess Rose makes the same mistake in *Baudoin de Sebourc*.
[15] In *Der grosse Wolfdietrich*, for example, the story of the hero's youth in exile is quite different.

la Duchesse,[16] which is believed by Heinzel to contain Frankish elements.[17] All this may be true; but too much importance must not be attached to the appearance of the ubiquitous accused wife and wicked major domo in any setting whatsoever. They are universally popular, not limited to the Franks.[18] *Parise la Duchesse* is indeed an analogous story, but so, as we have seen, are many others. Moreover, the exile of the heroine is brought about in an entirely different fashion.

Twelve traitors of the race of Ganelon, who have already killed her father, plan to destroy her as well for safety's sake. They send her some poisoned apples, which she innocently offers to her brother-in-law Boevon. She thus becomes seemingly responsible for his death. The accusation against her is treason.[19] She is condemned to die by fire; but, on her plea to live until her child is born, she is allowed to go into exile instead. Her son is born in the forests of Hungary, is taken from her by robbers and presented to the King of that country, and, like Esmoreit, falls in love with his foster sister when he is grown up. Like Esmoreit too he feels that his first and most pressing duty is to seek his parents. Some of Ganelon's omnipresent tribe call him a foundling, and he sets out to find his mother (who identifies him in Cologne by a birthmark on his shoulder), to convince his father of the injustice of his decree, and to reunite his parents. And he does all this before he marries his foster sister in Hungary.

If this *chanson de geste* has any connection with *Wolfdietrich*, it also diverges notably from the German. Instead of the love-smitten, revengeful seneschal, we have traitors of the race of Ganelon, no less than twelve; the motive is political, as it was in the Olive stories, not amorous; the accusation is treason, not infidelity; the child is born after the mother's exile and is not concerned in the accusation or disgrace of the mother, since his parenthood is never doubted; the Duke marries a relative of the chief villain, as in the Olive stories, instead of dying and leaving his wife to remarry as in *Wolfdietrich*. The whole action resembles the Olive-cycle rather than any other. Tomile, it will be remem-

---

[16] *Anciens Poetes de la France*, Paris, 1860.
[17] R. Heinzel: *Über die ostgothische Heldensage, Sitzungsberichte der k. Akademie der Wissenschaften*, CXIV, 1889, no. 3 (Philosophisch-historische Classe).

[18] This may not mean, of course, that the rest of the Hugdietrich-cycle may not be distinctively Frankish.
[19] The same accusation is brought against Guinevere in the *Mort Artu*.

bered, had wished the Duke to marry a relative of his, just as the Duke here is persuaded to marry a traitor's daughter after Parise has been sent away. The similarities which remain between *Parise* and *Wolfdietrich*—the birthmark of the hero, the exile of the Queen, her faithful friend, the restoration of mother and son— are commonplaces in this general type of story. Other pairs of narratives are more closely connected than these two. And a third romance, somewhat like *Parise*, varies still more from *Wolfdietrich*. In *Doon de Maience*,[20] the wicked and ambitious seneschal accuses the heroine of her husband's death, and tries to have her children murdered by their tutor. Her son Doon escapes, however, and returns just in time to save his mother from the death by fire to which she had been condemned for the second time. In *Charles le Chauve*,[21] likewise, a traitor causes the exile of the grandson of Charles by exposure, and young Dieudonné returns with an army just in time to effect a thrilling rescue of his mother from the same death. These rescue scenes are very often the most successful episodes in the romances they adorn, but they can not be considered anything but commonplaces of medieval fiction.

One of the many episodes of *Theseus de Cologne*, which is partly localized, like *Parise*, in that famous Rhine city, turns likewise on an accusation of treason. The motive for it is, however, the more usual resentment of a lover rebuffed.

Theseus, leaving Cologne to fight his vindictive old father-in-law, confides his wife Flore and the city to the care of the steward Melfior. This person follows the best romantic precedent by falling in love with his lady.

> fol. 96b   Yseut morut damours Jen vueil morir [aussy];
> Le saige aristote tout son sens y perdy,

he pleads. When she rejects his suit, he necessarily retracts and pretends that he only meant to test her fidelity to her husband. In revenge, he forges a treasonable correspondence between Flore and the enemy. Then he accuses her of treason before the assembled barons. She pleads her own version of the affair:

> fol. 98b   Pour dieu beau sires nen parlez ensement,
> Onques ne le pensay saches par mon serment . . .
> Se ma fait Melchior le traitre faillis,
> Qui lautrier me pris qu'il fut mes amis.

[20] Ed. M. A. Pey, Paris, 1859.
[21] The villain is a rejected lover who accuses the Queen of cannibalism. See Appendix II, 8.

When she is about to be burnt, like most damsels in her case, her husband arrives. He is as credulous as anyone concerning the slanders. But a certain goldsmith, a bourgeois friend of Theseus, offers combat in her behalf, and reproaches Theseus for his little faith in her integrity. After many days, the combat takes place; but a lacuna (of sense, not of script) occurs in the MS.[22] just before the gallant goldsmith draws his sword. We know from the corresponding passage in the folk-book that the amorous steward is defeated and forced to withdraw his accusation, so that Flore is freed of the charge of treason.

Romances like *Parise* and *Theseus* are interesting for another reason. The woes of these heroines are dwelt upon and enlarged in a style clearly intended to arouse the tears and sympathy of listeners. There is a striving after the emotional values which may be extracted from their situation. They are no longer mute victims of a mother-in-law's hatred, entirely passive as in the fairy tales and some of the romances. They have become alive, eloquent, and full of dignity. Before Parise goes into exile she insists upon entering her husband's castle at night to look upon him in silence. The scene is really affecting. Other treatments strive also to realize the dramatic and human possibilities of the accused queen; but very rarely, even then, is the repentance of her husband proportionate to the sympathy she has aroused.

Some of these stories have been distinguished by variety in the number of traitors. Parise was the victim of twelve; the Empress of Alemayn in some cases was the victim of two. A plurality of persecutors is rather awkward for a story-teller to manage, as we noticed in the legend of Valentine, where the mother-in-law was duplicated by a bishop. Another duplication, similar to that in the *Erl of Toulouse*, is contained in an episode of the *Ðidrekssaga*,[23] where Sisibe, the mother of Sigfroed (Sigurd) is the accused Queen, and the part of the wicked seneschal is taken by two men, Hermann and Hartvin. They are rejected in turn, compare notes, form an improbable alliance in evil, accuse Sisibe to her husband, and receive the royal command to put her to death in the forest. Here one of them kills the other, and Sisibe dies in giving birth to

---

[22] At the end of fol. 110.
[23] C. R. Unger, *Saga Ðiðriks Konungs af Bern*, Christiania, 1853, 157-170. The character of an accused queen, which is given to Sigfroed's mother here, is a new feature, probably due to the lost German original of the Saga; and even in that original it must have been a borrowed feature from romance sources.

her son. The presence of two unwelcome lovers instead of one may be explained in such cases by the well-known Biblical story of Susannah, the popularity of which is attested in the history of painting.[24]

C. THE LOVER AND DWARF AS ACCUSERS

Another group of romances[25] presents a new confederate for the villain: not a second lover, but a dwarf. These romances possess the stock features of a standard *chanson de geste* plot: the emphasized wickedness of the villain, the prominence given to the seneschal (which Heinzel attributes to the historical importance of the Merovingian major domo among the Franks), and the birth of the queen's child in exile under distressing circumstances.[26] Here the dwarf-tool of the villain is nearly always consciously bad like his master. The villain for whom *Macaire* is named (a member of Ganelon's accursed tribe) orders his dwarf to incriminate Queen Blanchefleur because he has been rejected by her. The dwarf acts his unpleasant part in full consciousness of its meaning. He also wishes to ruin Blanchefleur because she has hurt his dignity as an intermediary. In *Diu Künigin von Frankrîch*, on the other hand, the dwarf is a passive and innocent victim, whom the villain lays beside the sleeping Queen while he is also asleep.[27] In the Dutch folk-book[28] and Spanish prose romance about Sibille, both no doubt

---

[24] Some distressed heroines are compared to her. Genoveva was called "De nederlandsche Susanna" (in a list of books to be had of the publishing house I. C. Paemel, Ghent, contained in an edition of *Valentijn en Oursson*), and Aubert le Mire, *Fasti Belgici et Burgundice*, Brussels, 1622, also compares her to Susannah. The letter of Wimfeling compares Eugenia's situation to Susannah's: fol. 19a, "Quid namque Susanne contigit que nephas consimile exegisse putabatur . . ." Cf. also Chaucer, *Man of Law's Tale*, l. 541.

[25] The versions are:
Macaire, chanson de geste, ed. M. F. Guessard, Paris, 1866. The story also appears in the *Gesta Romanorum* and in the chronicle of Albericus Trium Fontium, ed. Leibnitz, II, Pt. 1, 105-106.
Diu Künigin von Frankrîch, von der Hagen's *Gesammtabenteuer*, I, 165-188.

Hystoria de la Reyna Sebilla, in the Spanish romance, *La Gran Conquista de Ultramar*. See Wolf, *Uber die neusten Leistungen der Franzosen*, 124-159.
Koningin Sibille, a Dutch folk-book. See *Denkschriften der k. Akademie der Wissenschaften*, Vienna, 1857, 180-282 (Philosophisch-historische Classe).
Sir Tryamour, a Middle English romance, Percy Society, London, 1846.

[26] This was apparently a very popular feature, deliberately used to arouse sympathy. Cf. *Aiol*, among others, where the heroine goes into exile with her husband, and is not accused herself; also *Lion de Bourges*.

[27] The villain is an unnamed Marshal, not related to Ganelon. The German romance diverges from the typically French characteristics throughout.

[28] No Middle Dutch romance is extant; but the existence of one can be inferred.

derived from a French folk-book, the dwarf is rejected with a blow on the mouth when he approaches the Queen,[29] and is therefore eager to ruin her even at the risk of his own life. But it is Macaire who pursues the exiled Queen, kills her faithful companion, and is identified and undone by the slain man's dog. The Dutch and Spanish treatments are diversified by the humorous exploits of the peasant Baroquel who rescues the Queen. He must have existed in the lost French source, since he appears also in the summary given in the chronicle of Albericus Trium Fontium, and in some fragments of a French poem on the subject.

The English romance *Sir Tryamour* varies from the other romances of this family in that it suppresses the dwarf entirely. Sir Marrok, the wicked steward, is the only villain. Yet *Sir Tryamour* undoubtedly belongs to the group in which a dwarf properly appears, since the rest of the plot, and especially the use of a dog as champion of virtue, corresponds to the others. Sir Marrok simply tells the King that the Queen has had a lover whom he has virtuously killed, and that the child she is expecting is illegitimate. He offers no proof, nor is any demanded by the credulous King. This whole group shows the usual traits of romance as opposed to fairy tales: motivation by a villain because of spurned love, use of combat as a means of vindicating virtue, the accusation of infidelity (and sometimes of illegitimacy as well). The special task given to the faithful dog has produced an additional change: the removal of the filial duty of championship from the son, who therefore becomes an inactive character in the tale of his mother's wrongs.

Without the preceding romances, we should probably not have the mosaic story of *Theseus de Cologne*,[30] part of which has already been discussed. The first part of the romance (which includes no less than three accused queens) concerns the fair Alidoyne, wife of Floridas, who is accused also of having a dwarf as lover. Her accuser is the typical rebuffed villain, but the dwarf is not only quite innocent, but her champion as well. The accusation here receives a certain color of probability from the aspect of the Queen's child, who is born small, ugly, and crippled; but that birth is ac-

See L. Petit, *Middelnederlandsche Bibl.*, I, 56.

[29] In the Dutch, Ch. 3: "hoe die naen der coninghinnen oneerbaerheyt te voren leyde, ende hoe si hem drie tanden wten hoofde sloech met haer vuyst."

[30] For summary, see Appendix II, no 4. The first pages of the MS. are defective; but their contents may be surmised from the prose folk-book.

counted for as in the Swan Children cycle: as a punishment from heaven because Alidoyne had mocked the mother of a similar child before the birth of her own (though here it is the ugliness of the one child, not the existence of twins, which makes the Queen suspect evil). Her punishment is carried out in the manner peculiar to the present cycle, by the accusations of a rejected lover, rather than the persecutions of a mother-in-law. The child helps to clear his mother's name, but he is not actually her champion. The unaided villainy of the lover here resembles that of other solitary evil doers like Tomile, Marrok, and Robbrecht. The *Theseus* episode illustrates the inexhaustible number of variations possible on the basic literary theme of an accused heroine.

D. PERSECUTORS IN PIOUS TALES

Another variation is the conversion of the heroine into a patient and long-suffering saint whose story is meant to convey religious edification. Such are Genevieve of Brabant, Hirlanda of Brittany, and Idda of Tockenburg. In the stories of these ladies, the villain's part is thoroughly conventional and romantic. These legends contain old and familiar elements, but their appearance in popular form was late. This is well known to be true of Genevieve of Brabant,[31] who has been discussed at greater length than Hirlanda and Idda. It seems probable that her story, like many others in the middle ages, originated in a monastery—Laach, 1325-1425?—as a means of glorifying its tradition and its founder. A Count of the Palatinate named Siegfried (died 1113) was a second founder of this monastery, and his name was evidently used as a center for fictional commonplaces about persecuted wives. The Rhineland and the Low Countries were especially kindly to such tales, as we have noticed, and so this tradition became popular there,[32] for the sake of the heroine rather than of the hero. It is

---

[31] Seuffert, *Die Legende von der Pfalzgräfin Genovefa*, Würzburg, 1877; B. Golz, *Pfalzgräfin Genoveva in der deutschen Dichtung*, Leipzig, 1897; H. W. Puckett, *The "Genoveva" Theme*, Mod. Phil., 1916, XIII, 609-624.

[32] Marquard Freher, following MSS. derived from Laach, incorporated it in the appendix of his *Origines Palatinae*,

1613. Bishop Matthias Emmich wrote the legend in Latin (edited in Latin and French by M. E. de la Bédollierre, Paris, 1841); but it first achieved popularity in the ornate version by the French Jesuit, René de Cerisiers (1603-1662): *L'Innocence Reconnue, ou la Vie de Sainte Genevieve de Brabant*, first datable print, 1638. In 1640 the same story was told

a very simple plot. The false seneschal Golo plays the usual part of lover and accuser, and Genevieve simply goes into exile to wait resignedly in the forest until her husband finds her. The accusation is not supported by a prepared scene with a supposed lover, as in the *Emperor Octavian*.[33] The child is entirely passive, and merely adds to the pathos of the situation. Golo himself is the beginning and end of the action, the clearest instance of the romantic traitor as rejected lover—the substitution of medieval romance for fairy-tale persecutors of more ancient date.

The story of Hirlanda of Brittany, published in 1640 as companion tale to *Genevieve of Brabant*,[34] is not so simple. In several features it reminds one of *Esmoreit* and the Swan Children cycle. In fact, like *Theseus de Cologne*, it seems to be a late composite of elements from several such tales.[35] The villain Gerard is simply another Robbrecht. His reason for hating Hirlanda is really ambition. He hates his infant nephew, her child, because he himself wishes to succeed his brother. He connives at the kidnapping of the child in order to put him out of the way, and to serve the purpose of a foreign king at the same time. Then he accuses Hirlanda of child-murder and infidelity. All of this is true in *Esmoreit*, with a few minor differences. In Hirlanda, however, the heroine's misadventure is uselessly duplicated. In both stories, her son is the rescuer. The boy's guardian learns of his ancestry here as does the hermit in the story of the Swan Children. None of the elements of the story is new; the whole is additional proof of the popularity of all of them.

The legend of St. Idda, more strictly local and ecclesiastical, takes us to the source of the Rhine. It is explicitly connected with

---

as one of three: *Les Trois États de L'Innocence Affligée dans Jeanne d'arc, Reconnue dans Genevieve de Brabant, Couronnée dans Hirlande, Duchesse de Bretagne.* A Dutch translation of Cerisiers' appeared in 1645, and in the eighteenth century came the Dutch and Flemish folk-books, which have remained popular to this day.

[33] In the best known versions, Golo uses a witch as confederate to support his accusation. But she is not a feature of the oldest forms of the story, and cannot therefore be compared to the waning witch-like mother-in-law of other stories.

[84] Also: *Hirlanda, die gekrönte Unschuld*, ca. 1700. (Title-page missing in the Brit. Mus. copy.) Summary in Appendix II, no. 5.

[35] The origin of the story, and its indebtedness to the romances, is discussed by Hermann Steinberger, *Hirlanda von Bretagne*, Munich, 1913. He points out the peculiarity of this plot in using ambition instead of scorned love as a motive (18-19).

the monastery of Fisching. The Latin *Vita* of 1685[36] mentions learned Latin histories which related the tale as fact. The legend merely tells how the heroine is basely accused by a courtier who hates her—"nescio, qua de causa," says the author. The only evidence is the presence of her wedding ring, which a crow had carried away, on the finger of a huntsman who had found it. Idda is thrown from a tower, but she miraculously survives and lives in the wilderness like Genevieve of Brabant, until she is found by her repentant husband. She does not return to him even after she has pardoned him, but retires to a religious retreat near the Benedictine Abbey of Fisching, where she often hears mass. Her miracles make the place famous.

This story is more successful as propaganda than as narrative. The villainy is quite unmotivated. In this respect, *Saint Idda* differs from *Genevieve*, which it most resembles. In all three, *Idda*, *Genevieve*, and *Hirlanda*, the character of the villain is crucial, and he does his evil work alone, like the truly romantic person he is.

E. The Brother-in-law as Accuser

One other solitary romantic villain remains to be discussed. This is the brother-in-law of the heroine who, in a numerous and popular cycle named from the Crescentia-version, accuses her of infidelity because, as in other groups, she has been obliged to cut short his wooing during her husband's absence. He does not present evidence to support his accusation. The heroine's exile is always diversified by many thrilling adventures, which were occasionally borrowed to adorn entirely independent narratives. One usual feature of an accused queen's exile is, however, lacking: she does not have a child. Nevertheless she is most emphatically the victim of accusations, like so many of her sisters.

Although the Crescentia-plot is not simple, it can be resolved into several formulae, some of which are common in fairy tales.

---

[36] *Vita et Confraternitas S. Jddae Comitissae Tockenburgi cum genealogijs illustrissimorum comitum de Tockenburg.* ... Constantiae, Anno MDCLXXXV. In 1481, a German Life was translated into Latin by Albert of Bonstetten, who later retranslated his little book "in elegantiorem vernaculam." In 1596, another German version appeared: *Kurze Beschreibung von dem Leben/ und Wandel/ der gottseligen Frauwen S. Idda Gräffin von Kirchberg u. So inn dem Würdigen Gottshaus Vischingen seliglich ruwet . . . Allen frommen Ehefrawen zu Trost vnd Exempel ganz nutzlich vnd kurzweilig zulesen. Erstmals in Truck fürgestellt.* Getrückt zu Freyburg in Vchtland, MDXCVI.

Wallensköld maintained[37] that the story is of Oriental origin and goes back to an hypothetical Indian source, inferred from the *Tūtī Nāmeh* of Nachshabī in the fourteenth century, from Arabic interpolations in the *Thousand and One Nights*, and from the story of Repsima in the Persian *Thousand and One Days*. Stefanović,[38] on the other hand, points out that these versions are all much later than the oldest European one, and that there is a considerable group of European fairy tales which contain parallels to a very characteristic incident: the bloody dagger used to implicate the heroine in a charge of murder. He points out that the number of persecutors is greatest in the Eastern versions, and that simplification would not be likely in the supposedly derivative Western versions: rather, that simplicity is a sign of antiquity. He stresses also those features of the Hildegard sub-group (such as general similarity to the Snow-White type of fairy tale) which suggest Germanic sources; and he connects the much-debated *Banished Wife's Lament* in Old English with this cycle of romances.[39] How far all this may be valid is of course unsettled; but the comparison with fairy tales, which Wallensköld had neglected, is very valuable indeed.

The oldest known literary version goes by the name of *Crescentia*,[40] and was written in Middle High German of the mid-twelfth century.

It tells how Crescentia of Rome, besieged by her brother-in-law's wooing, commands him to build a tower for them before she will consent; how she cleverly contrives his incarceration in this same tower, but rashly sets him free on the day of her husband's return; how she is thrown into the Tiber by her husband, who believes the accusation brought against her by his brother; how a spurned lover in the court where she finds

---

[37] *Le Conte de la Femme Chaste convoitée par son Beau-Frere*, in: *Acta Societatis Scientiarum Fennicae*, XXXIV, no. 1; also his introduction to *Florence de Rome* for the Soc. des An. Textes Fr. Cf. also R. Köhler, *Archiv für Lit.-geschichte*, XII, 92-148.

[38] *Rom. Forschungen*, XXIX, 461-556.

[39] For an interpretation connecting this *Lament* with the Constance-cycle—a more likely connection, it seems to me—see W. W. Lawrence in *Mod. Phil.*, V, 1908, 387-406.

[40] *Kaiserchronik*, ed. H. F. Massmann, Quedlinburg, 1854, ll. 11,367-12,828. Von der Hagen, *Gesammtabenteuer*, I, 129-164; edited and revised by Oskar Schade, Berlin, 1853. A later, thirteenth-century form is given by Von der Hagen, I, Intro., c. Prose versions: *Altdeutsche Blätter*, I, 300-308; *Die deutschen Mundarten*, II, 7; the prose redaction of the *Kaiserchronik*.. As a folk-book, only in the nineteenth century (ed. Schönhuth, 1864).

refuge accuses her of murdering her fosterling, and she is cast into the water again because the testimony of the bloody dagger by her side seems conclusive; and how finally all of her persecutors, struck by punitive maladies, come to be cured by her healing power, which was granted to her by St. Peter after her many sufferings. She heals her persecutors after they have made full confession. So the truth is made manifest, and she retires to a convent with her name cleared.

The plot-scheme of this early treatment holds for succeeding versions: exile caused by the accusation of a rejected brother-in-law, a varying number of persecutions and sufferings, and a healing of her persecutors after they have confessed their sins. The use of a bloody dagger by one of the persecutors has already appeared in certain fairy tales and in the Chaucer-group of the Constance-saga. In the latter, it is true, there is an important difference, since the murdered victim is the wife, not the child, of the protector of Constance. In one group of Crescentia-tales, the emphasis is laid on the saint-like character of the lady, and on the miraculous means of her restoration. The group is made up of plays and edifying legends[41] which are likewise quite simple in plot; though the opening varies considerably, the brother-in-law is usually the persecutor[42] who is punished by disease and healed by the miraculous powers of her whom he has wronged. Another group is less pious and more romantic and martial. The chief representatives of the story in this division center about the French romance *Florence de Rome*.[43] This group results from the dilution of the essential plot with medieval ingredients: fights with the heathen, cities besieged for the sake of a fair princess, knightly combats, ladies watching from the castle walls. The marriage of

---

[41] The version of the story told by Vincent of Beauvais as a miracle of the Virgin (*Spec. Hist.*, VII, 90-92) was very popular. Jacob van Maerlant retold it from Vincent (Pt. I, Bk. VII, Ch. 45). Here the episode of the child-murder is retained; it is dropped from the French miracle play. In the Italian group (a fifteenth-century poem edited by A. Mussafia: *Sitzungsberichte der k. Akademie der Wissenschaften*, Vienna, II, 589 ff., and the Vita and play about St. Guglielma) there is no tower episode, and new introductions are provided. Gautier de Coinsi's poem (M. Méon, *Nouveau Recueil de Fabliaux et Contes*, Paris, 1823,

II, 1-128) contains both the murder and the tower.

[42] In the Italian poem, edited by Mussafia, the villain is a nephew, and the rejected lover who murders the child is also a nephew of the child's father. An Italian novella of the fourteenth century (*Novelle d'Incerti Autori del Secolo XIV*, Bologna, 1861) combines the brother-in-law episode with the murder of the child, and makes the child the heroine's own. This results in the old primitive accusation of having murdered her own child.

[43] For the Middle English romance see *Le Bone Florence de Rome*, ed. by Vietor and Knobbe, Marburg, 1899.

Florence to Esmere occurs during the bustle and clamor of a war against the besieger, Garcy of Constantinople; and it is to pursue this Garcy that Esmere leaves his wife to the guardianship and persecutions of his brother Miles. Her later adventures include not only the usual accusation of having murdered her infant charge, but narrow escapes from other amorous or covetous persecutors as well. In this French romance and in *Le Dit de Flourence de Rome*[44] (early fourteenth century), there is a deliberate heightening of effects by familiar methods in order to arouse sympathy for the unhappy exiled lady. The *Dit* is more labored than the romance in its straining after excitement and sympathy.

The *Gesta Romanorum* also contains a version of this pathetic tale,[45] which provided the source for Thomas Hocleve's *Fabula de quadam Imperatrice Romana*.[46] In both of these, the heroine endures a variety of persecutions during her exile; but she is not actually accused by the brother-in-law to her husband. She is directly wronged, not slandered. In the Hildegard group,[47] however, her husband (Charlemagne) listens to accusations from his brother Talandus, and gives orders himself for her exposure in the forest. This particular form of the legend is simpler than most, because it lacks the usual persecutions from the child-murderer, the ungrateful youth saved from the gallows, and the amorous mariner, which are to be found in other versions. It ends with the usual scene of reunion brought about by the heroine's cures. The story was believed by some writers to be historical, and was introduced into chronicles, sermons, and old histories, especially from the chronicle of the Abbey of Kempten, written by the Bavarian Johannes Birck.

[44] A. Jubinal, *Nouveau Recueil des Contes, Dits, Fabliaux . . . des 13-15 Siècles*, Paris, 1839, 88-117. Here, the advent of the two brothers is not prepared for, as in the romance. Names appear abruptly throughout, as if the poem were somewhat unskillfully condensed. The woes of the heroine are partly attributed to her breaking a vow not to marry. Her brother-in-law does not accuse her, but subjects her to mistreatment from which she is rescued. Her persecutor at the home of her rescuer is called *Macaire*—a name elsewhere associated with the molesters of innocent ladies. See Von der Hagen, *Gesammtabenteuer*, I, civ.

[45] Ed. J. G. T. Grässe, Leipzig, 1842, II, 152, no. 87. In the English *Gesta*, Ed. Sir F. Madden, no. 69, the Emperor is called "Merelaus" instead of "Octavianus."

[46] EETS, London, 1892, I, 140.

[47] Wallensköld, Introduction; K. Reiser, *Sagen, Gebräuche und Sprichwörter des Allgäus*, I, 442; Bäckström, *Svenska Folkböcker*, I, 264-271; Belg. Museum, III, 241.

The Crescentia-story appeared in Middle Dutch in a form which has the distinction of being generally neglected by those who have discussed the cycle as a whole. Perhaps it has been overlooked because it forms part of the long patchwork epic, *Seghelijn van Jerusalem*,[48] and the Crescentia-patch appears near the end. The poem is apparently not translated from any other language,[49] and may be called an original work as it stands, even though much of it is plainly modeled on known French romances. At his best, the author writes in a fresh and vivid style that makes events concretely visible; but he is not always able to bring a logical relationship into the events he combines from his various sources. The passage in question here is a good example of the strength and weakness of his work. The heroine is sent into exile by a villain who is not a brother-in-law, although all of his actions have been borrowed from brothers-in-law, in the kindred cycle. Her persecution at the court of her first protector is modified to an accusation of poisoning, much as in the *chanson de geste Parise la Duchesse*.[50] She is condemned to die by fire, but spared at last for exile, like Parise. She bears a child alone in the forest without help. This scene is almost certainly due to romances like *Parise*. But in the succeeding adventures with the ungrateful youth saved from the gallows and the amorous mariner, the child is completely forgotten and reappears only at the end, when the cures and reconciliations take place. His casual appearance and disappearance result from the combination of two alien plots; but such inconsistencies weigh little in comparison with the unforced charm and gaiety of the scene in which Florette plays unwittingly with the poisoned pear, while the mirthful young knight Antidotes tries to win it from her. The romance is written with liveliness and originality, even if the multiple themes from French romance are imperfectly combined. If the genial author drew directly from French sources, as he not improbably did, his work suggests a typical channel through which accused queens of the civilized *chanson de geste* type entered the vernacular literature of the Low Countries. Whether or not

---

[48] Ed. Verdam, Leiden, 1878, 94 ff.
[49] *Ibid.*, v.
[50] These lines particularly recall Parise:
9220 Florette die stont al bevende
　　　Van groeter pine in haer gedoech.

Tkint in haren buke vloech,
Daer ment toesaech, op ende neder.
Sebastiaen seide, "Nu leit weder
Die vrouwe in den kerker dijn . . .
9233 Wat heeft ons dat kint misdaen?"

he actually drew on *Parise*, does not matter. Something of the sort he surely did use, subject to the modifications of his own creative fancy. And this was happening in the fourteenth century, about the time of the composition of *Esmoreit* in the same country. So we gain, perhaps, some little insight into the possibilities for the genesis of the Netherlandish drama. It too has a plot compounded of several commonplaces of romance, probably derived from French models, and probably put together with a certain freedom. And *Esmoreit* also, on a smaller scale, results in an illogical plot because the weaving is not quite skilful enough.

SUMMARY

The stories discussed in this chapter illustrate the final stages of a process of plot-evolution. They employ uniformly the more advanced types of motivation: an ambitious or a love-sick villain uttering accusations of infidelity or treason. The change is unmistakable; and this later plot-machinery has become thoroughly conventional, being used again and again in repetitions of which medieval audiences never wearied.

Let us recapitulate the entire process as it has been revealed in this study. In folk-tales, queens are accused of strange, incredible crimes: cannibalism, witchcraft, child-murder, the birth of animals. The accusers and persecutors are demons, witches, fathers, mothers-in-law, and stepmothers. In romances, several of these motives reappear, much as they exist in folk-tales. But some romances, like *Octavian* and *Valentine*, present a combination of märchen motives like these with others apparently more romantic and sophisticated: the jealousies and desires of court intrigue. The combination seems to indicate a transition. Moreover, certain definite story-cycles, which have been preserved both in older and more recent stages of development, show the actual process of dropping the märchen machinery in favor of more modern devices. Thus, in the Swan Children story and in *Valentine*, one can see primitive persecutors and accusations (mothers-in-law, animal birth, and child-murder) being supplanted by more modern ones (courtiers, like Macaire and the Bishop; treason; or infidelity). Finally, the greater number of romances limit themselves to persecution by a villain instead of a demonic or tribal tyrant, and the accusation of treason or infidelity is the weapon used against innocence. The two changes occur simultaneously. The villain, typical of the latest stage, is often of the race of Ganelon,[51] and he works either for the sake of ambition or for the satisfaction of revenge for rejected love. His behavior is conventional and calculable enough, and is common in the fiction of our own times.

Chaucer's Constance and the Queen in *Esmoreit* are, therefore, far from unique in character and situation. Other queens have, like Constance, been accused of the birth of monsters; queens other than Esmoreit's mother have been accused of child-murder or an illicit love affair; others have been rescued from prison or exile by their grown children; others have suffered these things at the hands of a mother-in-law or a scheming villain. Donegild in Chaucer belongs to the Matabrune-type; Robbrecht in *Esmoreit* belongs to the Macaire-type, common in the *chansons de geste,* though it is not so clear in the play why the Queen's destruction is necessary to him. Take him away and we have simply the formula of the exposed or persecuted child, who suffers because a great king fears him. The presence of this formula in märchen and romance suggests another study: an inquiry into the reasons for the exposure or persecution of a child, in the light of folk-lore and obsolescent custom. It would no doubt yield illuminating results concerning the origin and development of tales about foundlings and exiled princes, no less interesting than the results presented here from a study of accused queens. Certainly the romances in which the persecuted mother of an exposed child is made the central sympathetic figure have a warmth and charm that is lacking in the more martial, exciting romances where her son becomes the chief character. That is why even the minor analogues of Chaucer's *Man of Law's Tale* are worthy of study if one would gain insight into one of the most attractive types of medieval romance.

[51] See Ernst Sauerland, *Ganelon und sein Geschlecht im altfranzöischen Epos,* Margurb, 1886.

APPENDICES

APPENDIX I

ADDITIONAL ANALOGUES OF *ESMOREIT*

The plot of the Flemish play *Esmoreit*, which contains the conventional characters of accused queen, scheming villain, persecuted child, and credulous husband, is composed of incidents which became commonplaces of medieval fiction. The following additional analogues will indicate the prevalence of these conventional motives:

1. The King of Damascus tries to prevent his daughter's marriage according to the prophecy.—In other words, Damiet is regarded to a certain extent as a Danaë whose future husband is the enemy of her father. Such situations are frequent in fairy tales, and they appear in romances again and again. The father surrounds the marriage of his daughter with difficulties, kills her suitors, persecutes his son-in-law, or exiles his grandson as the monarchs of fairy tales are wont to do. The Danaë situation is traceable in: *Richars li Biaus*, the Middle Dutch play *Gloriant*, the Dutch folk-book *Turias ende Florete*, *Hugdietrich*, *Torrent of Portyngale*, *Sir Eglamour*, *Sir Degarre*, *Amadis de Gaul*, *Theseus de Cologne* (see Appendix II), the Dutch folk-book *Malegijs* (in the part concerning the hero's brother Vivian), *Boeve de Hamptone*, the *Dit de l'Empereur Constant*, and the innumerable other members of the cycle in which an exchanged letter saves the life of the future son-in-law.[1] Not all of these romances, however, use a prophecy to initiate the persecution. In one interesting case, the prophecy is employed to warn the hero's *father* of doom at his son's hands. This Oedipus-situation is to be found in *Seghelijn van Jerusalem* (see Appendix II, no. 7); and the scene in which the court astrologer reads the doleful prophecy in the stars is very similar to the one in *Esmoreit* between the heathen King and Meester Platus.

2. The hero is exposed or sold by the villain, or is otherwise persecuted, because he interferes with the latter's ambition.—Analogues to this situation occur in: *Theseus de Cologne*, *Historia Meriadoci*,[2] *Seghelijn*, *Guillaume de Palerne*, *Doon de Maience*, *Jourdains de Blaivies*, *Aiol*, *Baudoin de Sebourc*, *Herzog Herpin*, *Floriant et Florete*, *Malegijs*, *Boeve de Hamptone*, and *Sir Generides*. The villains of these stories are of the conventional French type, sometimes definitely related to Ganelon.

---

[1] See *Romania*, VI, 161 ff.; R. Köhler, *Zur erzählenden Dichtung des Mittelalters*, 355 ff.; Josef Schick, *Corpus Hamleticum*, I, Berlin, 1912.

[2] Ed. James D. Bruce, *Hesperia*, Ergänzungsreihe, 2 Heft, 1913.

Jan uut den Vergier[3] contains a son exiled by his own father and persecuted by a villain. The similarity of some sections of this folk-book to *Esmoreit*, and the occurrence of passages of verbal similarity, have led Priebsch[4] to the conclusion that the material of *Jan* served directly to furnish out the plot of *Esmoreit*. It must be confessed that the very rhymes correspond closely in the passage resembling Esmoreit's outburst to Damiet when he discovers that he is a foundling; but the exclamations of all exposed princes on such occasions are very similar and highly conventional. Lines 1238 ff. of the Low German *Valentine* are also very similar to Esmoreit's and Jan's speeches under like circumstances, but in other respects all three plots are very dissimilar. I do not think it likely that *Jan* alone is so important in explaining *Esmoreit*.

3. The hero, a foundling, falls in love with his foster sister.—This very common situation occurs in: *Jan uut den Vergier, Malegijs, Boeve de Hamptone, Guillaume de Palerne, Theseus de Cologne* (the Gadifer and Osanne episode), *Renier, Charles le Chauve*, and with slight modifications, in *Baudoin de Sebourc, Richars li Biaus*, and *Ogier the Dane*. Very frequently in these the foundling's clothes bring about his identification.

A popular prose tale of the fifteenth century in Flanders attaches such a foundling story to the family of St. Louis of France.[5] It is told that the consort of St. Louis, while she was crusading with her husband, bore a son named Jehan-Tristan. A Saracen woman acting as a spy steals the child out of the city of Damietta and delivers him to the Sultan Saladin of Turkey, who gives out that the boy is his son. So Jehan-Tristan grows up to fight against his own relatives. One day when he is about to enter combat with his uncle Charles of Sicily, he notices that both of them are being held back by an invisible force. An angel descends from heaven to reveal his ancestry to Jehan-Tristan. He is converted on the spot, returns home, is reunited to his mother, and returns to the East to fetch the fair Helaine who had loved him when she had believed him to be her cousin.

Here, attached to historical personages, we have a story very close to *Esmoreit*, except for the villain Robbrecht, who, we have elsewhere decided, is a detachable romantic character in the midst of other material. And geographically also *Le Livre de Baudoyn* is important. It represents a popular sort of pseudo-history, really crusading romance, current in the Low Countries which produced *Esmoreit* about the same time, and other tales like it. It features conspicuously the siege of Damietta in Egypt, where the fabulous Jehan-Tristan was supposedly kidnapped. Now the

---

[3] *Sammlung bibliothekswissenschaftlicher Arbeit*, Leipzig, 1895, VIII, 1-23. The folk-book is evidently based on a lost poem in Middle Dutch, since the prose retains traces of rhyme and rhythm. The poem probably belonged to the time and style of *Seghelijn*. There is a Middle High German poem on the same subject.

[4] *Neophilologus*, VII, 57-62.

[5] *Le Livre de Baudoyn, Conte de Flandre*, Brussels, 1836 (republished from the 1485 edition), 150 ff.

heroine of *Esmoreit* bears the name of that city, which was such a strategic point for the crusaders; and one can easily imagine that her name—or its name—was very often on people's lips in the Netherlands, since a detachment of Dutch-speaking soldiers under Count William of Holland was very active at the siege of 1218-1219. Indeed, the word for a bell is *damiet* to this day, because of the bells which were brought home from the siege as trophies. It is not strange, therefore, to find a character named Damiet in a story which obviously took its present form under the influence of crusading romances and *chansons de geste* in general. The heathen princess of *Esmoreit*, moreover, is closely paralleled by the Saracen Helayne in *Le Livre de Baudoyn*. This book suggests not only the presence of enlightening analogues to *Esmoreit* in the popular literature of the Low Countries, but also the geographical origin and diffusion of them.

4. Sicily is the scene of part of the action.—Many of the tales already mentioned are staged on this attractive island: *Floriant et Florete, Renier, Maugis d'Aigremont, Dolopathos, Charles le Chauve, Lion de Bourges*; also *Ipomedon, Prothesileus*, and parts of *Jourdains de Blaivies, Enfances Garin de Montglane, Tristan de Nantueil*, and *Le Livre de Baudoyn*. The reasons for this romantic and literary interest in Sicily[6] are probably geographic again, because the crusading expeditions of Western Europe brought many individuals to that island where poetry and storytelling were so diligently fostered by the successive dynasties ruling there. Many an expedition against Damietta, composed of Sicilian Normans and soldiers from Northern Europe—Dutch and Flemish among others—departed from Sicily. All of these connections are vague enough, but they do serve to bring together such names as Sicily, Flanders, Damietta, and the Saracens. It is not at all strange that Sicily should be chosen as the scene of a Flemish play of the late fourteenth century, which is full of the spirit of the crusades, and contains a character named Damiet, an accused queen, an exiled son, and a Saracen king as foster father—especially if that play reached Flanders by way of France and French literature. As for the popularity of such themes in the Netherlands and Rhineland, we have already had abundant evidence of that in the versions of *La Belle Hélène, Valentine, Theseus de Cologne, Doon de la Roche, Parise la Duchesse, Baudoin de Sebourc, Seghelijn, Le Livre de Baudoyn, Jan uut den Vergier, Olive, Malegijs, Genoveva of Brabant, Moriaen*, and *De Ridder metter Mouwe*, which circulated in these parts or localized their action there.

[6] I have already discussed one phase of it in *The Romanic Review*, XIV, 168-188.

APPENDIX II

SUMMARIES OF ROMANCES

1. *La Belle Hélène de Constantinople*, MS. 9967 in the Bibliothèque Royale, Brussels. This prose version of the poem was made by Jean Wauquelin in 1448. The codex is beautifully lettered in clear characters, and adorned with decorated capitals and pictures from the story. Jean dedicates his translation to "Phillipe par la Grace de dieu duc de bourgoinge de loth*ringen* de brabant et de lembourg. Conte de flandres dartois de bourg*oigne* palatin de hayn*ault*, de holland de zeelande et de namur Marquis du saint empire seigneur de frise de Salmes et de Malines." It was especially in the low-lying, Germanic-speaking sections of these possessions that the story became most popular later in the form of folk-books.

The folk-books listed by Florian Forcheur (*Messager des Sciences Historiques de Belgique*, Ghent, 1846, pp. 169-209) are but a part of those still extant. A very cursory search in the libraries of Holland and Belgium reveals many more, especially Dutch ones. One popular book combined the tale of Helena with two others: *De Vrouwenperle ofte dryvoudige Historie van Helena de Verduldige, Griseldis de Saechtmoedige, Florentina de Getrouwe*, Antwerp, 1621 (modern reprint, Harlem, 1910).

Neither poem nor prose version has been published. The story runs thus: Hélène's mother dies, leaving her father, the Emperor of Constantinople, disconsolate. He loves his daughter more deeply than ever in his sorrow. When Hélène is grown, the devil turns the Emperor's affection into unlawful love. The Emperor serves the Pope in war against the heathen, but demands in return a dispensation permitting him to marry his own daughter. When he arrives in Constantinople, he is received by Hélène "comme celle qui a autre chose ne pensoit fort que a tout honneur et a tout bien, ne iamais neust pense que son pere lempereur fust en celle erreur en laquelle il estoit quant il se partist." [1] She is soon confronted with the truth. Her father confides her to the care of a certain Dame Beatrix who, instead of guarding her, allows her to escape. A friendly mariner conveys her "au bort de la mer en ung pays nom*me* pour le temps vaute*n*bron Mais comme dist no*str*e hystoire on le appelle maintenant la marche de flandres." [2] Here she takes refuge in a convent; but the wooing of the then pagan King of Flanders causes her to flee once more. On the way, she is temporarily endangered by an amorous pirate, who is opportunely drowned in the storm which casts her ashore in England, near the King's castle. King Henry finds her, and

[1] Fol. 21a.   [2] Fol. 25b.

falls in love with her. He marries her in spite of his mother's objection to her as a *fille esgarée*.

The King's mother is thus characterized: "Cestui noble roy auoit une mere qui ia estoit tres ancienne et estoit de tres malle nature car a nul bien fait apienne pouoit elle entendre." [3] And she warns her son before the marriage: "Je vous prometz par la foi que dois adieu mon createur se vous le faictes iamais a moy naurez paix ne elle aussi." He replies to all aspersions on Hélène that she would be worthy of the marriage even if she were the daughter of the poorest man in the world, being what she is. When he goes to war, he leaves his wife in care of the Duke of Gloucester. The mother-in-law visits Hélène long enough to have a counterfeit seal made. With this she seals the substituted letters which she gives to the drunken messenger. The chaplain who writes from her dictation the accusation of a monstrous birth, protests against the lie. She silences him with money, and, when the letter is written, cuts his throat.

In Rome, King Henry has learned of his wife's ancestry and her relationship to the Pope, by pictures of her which he finds there. When the forged letter reaches them, the Pope shrewdly asks whether Hélène has incurred the enmity of anyone in England on account of her marriage. Henry tells about his mother; and the Pope suggests the message in return, asking the Duke of Gloucester to guard the Queen. This second letter is changed to a command to burn mother and children. The Duke says, "Affin que quant monsieur le roy retournera nous lui monstrons aucune chose de vostre noble corps. Je vous Trencheray ung bras deuant et en presence de tous ceulx qui cy sont." [4] The daughter of the Duke, Marie, offers to be burnt instead of Hélène, and they actually agree. So an arm is cut off Marie too, and the Queen's arm is attached to one of the two children when they are set afloat with their mother.

When Henry returns he traces the deceit to its source, and has his mother's head cut off. Hélène's father comes to England searching for her, and joins her husband in his quest. From this moment the plot becomes repetitious and long-winded to wearisomeness. Henry recognizes his two sons in Tours because of the embalmed hand of their mother which they still carry with them. Hélène is also in Tours at the time; but she leaves before they find her. She leads them a pretty dance up and down Europe and back to Tours again, evidently fearing that the mood of her father and husband has not changed. Finally, after many alarms, pursuits, and escapes, she is discovered in Tours once more. Her hand is restored to her arm by prayer; she cries her husband mercy for the great travail she has caused him. Her attitude is surprisingly humble, when one considers that she still thinks he wrote the second substituted letter. However, explanations follow simply enough. Hélène's son Martin becomes the successor of his patron the Archbishop of Tours.

[3] Fol. 33a. [4] Fol. 56b.

2. *Theseus de Cologne*, MS. Brit. Mus. Add. 16,955. The section which resembles the Swan Children cycle begins on fol. 161b. Gadifer, son of Theseus, has grown up with Osanne, his foster sister. He marries her after he has been told that he is a foundling, but before he knows that he is of royal ancestry. Later, when he has defeated his enemies and regained his heritage, he takes his humble wife with him as Empress. But Clodas, the widow of one of his enemies, wishes to usurp the place of Osanne in order to rehabilitate her fallen fortunes. She uses the mechanism of a conventional fairy-tale mother-in-law. When she hears that the Empress has borne three children during her husband's absence, Clodas removes them and substitutes puppies. The infants are given to a bribed confederate to be "killed in some forest or cast into some river"; but they are exposed instead. It will be necessary, says Clodas, to tell the Emperor

Que de chiens se laissa vo moulier habiter Et tant vous en dy bien ne le vous doy celer Que vous ferez vostre nom abaisser & blasmer Si jamais la lessez auec vous demourer.[5]	que la dame sest deliuree de trois chiens et que ung chien les a conceuz et engendriez en la dame.[6]

The Emperor accepts her theory. He orders his wife into prison, and curses the hour of their marriage. "For he who gave her to me knew of a truth that I was of high and royal line, and he made her my wife that his line might be exalted and his daughter rise to high estate, which was a great wrong to me." Osanne is exiled after a term in prison. Her absence gives the wicked Clodas her opportunity. She throws herself constantly in Gadifer's way:

La royne Clodas la fit moult varier Et se mectoit en lieu chambre & en solier Ou le roy ne pouoit contrester ne laisser.[7]	Il nalloit en nul lieu feust en chambre ou en salle que il ne trouuast tousiours la mauuaise femme Clodas deuant luy.[8]

And she does succeed in captivating him, "for when a woman wishes to spread her nets to catch and deceive a man, it is marvel indeed if he escape unless he takes flight entirely from such folk," says the author of the prose book. However, the ambition of Clodas is not gratified by marriage with the Emperor.

Meantime a charcoalburner named Renier has found the three exposed boys. He joyfully displays them to his wife, who for her part objects that they will be a great burden and little profit. The honest Renier promises that he will eat and drink less to make up for the expense, and that he will abstain from the tavern until the boys are ten years old. His wife accepts the offer, but threatens to expose the foundlings once more if he breaks his promise.

[5] *Chanson de geste*, fol. 164a.
[6] Folk-Book, ed. Paris, ca. 1530, fol. 170a.
[7] *Chanson de geste*, fol. 166a.
[8] Folk-Book, fol. 174a.

Le gentis charbonniers les ama et tint cher
Ne onques puis nosa sa femme couroucer
Et quant sa femme le voit esmaier
Les iii enfans portoit pardessus ung fumier.[9]

Et quant la preudefemme le vouloit bien esmayer ou couroucer elle portoit les trois enfans dessus ung fumier ou faisoit semblant de les rapporter au bois.[10]

From that day the good man is entirely ruled by his wife, who employs the threat with great effect. But at least the children have an asylum. When they are grown up, they take service under their own father, rescue him in combat with the heathen, and are knighted by him. Their material rewards they divide with the honest charcoalburner, who is delighted with them. But the wicked Clodas notices their resemblance to the Emperor, and suspects who they are. So she mixes poison in some wine, and bids a page carry it to the Emperor, saying that the three young champions have sent it. The squire who tastes it for the Emperor dies; the Emperor casts the three accused youths into prison. The gallant Renier thereupon offers himself as champion to fight Richier, knight of Clodas. Of course the just side wins; Richier confesses complicity to the crime, Clodas is sentenced, the baby-clothes of the foundlings are produced, and the Emperor joyfully recognizes his sons. But many years and many adventures intervene before he finds his wife Osanne in Jerusalem, where, as in the Old French play, she had taken refuge.

3. *Doon de la Roche*, MS. Brit. Mus. Har., 4404.—Doon l'Alemant is rewarded by Pippin for long service by marriage with his sister Olive. The two have a son named Landri. Their happiness is interrupted by Tomile of Cologne, a descendant of Ganelon. This person takes Doon aside and whispers to him

fol. 3b Madame ne uous aimme vallisant . I . bouton;
Iermain la pris prouee gisant a . i . garcon.

Doon sternly bids the slanderer hold his peace, but Tomile persists in his unexplained hostility to Olive. He bids a young man of the court lie beside her in her room, where she is stupified from a drink Tomile has given her. The youth is tempted by the bribes offered, and goes. Doon is called in to see the prepared scene, and the unhappy youth is punished immediately with death. Olive wakes. Doon is restrained with difficulty from executing her as well. She offers to endure various tests of her innocence. His answer is not very logical: "Mauuaise die li duc pour quoi parles tant?" As he leaves the chamber he meets his young son, whom he strikes cruelly. Pippin is summoned to Cologne; Olive repeats her offer:

fol. 8a He dex ia suis ie preste de mise porter,
Soit en feu ou en eaue ou la ou[11] vous uoudres.

[9] *Chanson de geste*, fol. 163b.
[10] Folk-Book, fol. 171b.
[11] MS., laiou.

But in spite of her offers and the protests of a few knights, Landri and his mother are disowned by Doon and Pippin. She is kept under guard, and Tomile promptly begins to urge Doon to marry his daughter. Pippin consents to this second marriage of Doon, provided his sister is well cared for. Young Landri goes to the wedding and cries out manfully:

> fol. 13b Sire duc de la roche gra*n*t pechie i aues,
> Qui ma dame lassies, aultre fame p*r*enes,
> fol. 14a Et moi toles ma te*rr*e et aultrui la donnes:
> Ma dame est toute p*r*este di mise porter,
> Soit en feu ou e*n* eue ou la ou vo*us* voudres.

Olive is also present, but mother and son only rouse Doon to taunt and disown them. Olive faints. Landri exchanges blows with Tomile. Doon interposes, and commands the two intruders to go back to their hostel.

Audegour, Doon's new wife, begins to work immediately against Landri. As she herself says, rather inelegantly,

> fol. 18a Je ne verai la*n*dri q*ue* na*n* aie duel ou va*n*tre.

She also objects to Olive's comparative freedom. She bears a son who calls Landri *Bastard* as soon as he is old enough. This taunt brings about a fight in which the older generation becomes involved. Such scenes as this cause Doon to urge the departure of Landri, for the boy's own safety. Landri goes to Paris, but he is repudiated by Pippin at the gates, and so he proceeds to Constantinople. Here he fights in a tournament, where he wins the love of the Emperor's daughter Salmadrine. The Emperor does not entirely approve of his daughter's choice, because Landri's ancestry is unknown, both parenthood and unclehood!

> fol. 29a Mais il ne scauoit mie cui fut filz ne cui nies

He sends messengers to France to ask Pippin about Landri's status. Salmadrine intercepts them and commands them, with vigorous threats, to bring back the kind of answer she wants. They hastily agree.

Meantime Audegour's son has begun to work against Olive and Doon. Olive is sent into exile, and Doon finds himself locked out of his own city, with the humiliating command to follow her in her disgrace. Doon replies,

> fol. 42b Elle ne fut onq*ues* pute ie le scai de uerite.

He retires into Hungary. While he is serving the Hungarian King, he is sent on an expedition against Constantinople, where he fights against his own son and is captured. Landri has decided that he must go home and reëstablish his mother; but the recognition by his father occurs first, and also his marriage to Salmadrine. Then father and son depart together to punish the evil ones at home. This process is long and exciting. Tomile confesses everything after his defeat. Olive and Doon are remarried.

APPENDICES 125

4. *Theseus de Cologne:* the accusation of Queen Alidoyne and the dwarf.—This episode comes at the beginning of the story. The first pages of the MS. are missing, but the faithful prose folk-book supplies their contents.

King Floridas of Cologne is summoned one day to the castle window by his wife Alidoyne. She has just seen a woman go by with a child "nain & bossu & le plus contrefait & le plus malforme que onques dieu crea sur terre."[12] She laughs mockingly and remarks that such offspring must be the result of infidelity. God is angry, and sends her in punishment a child as ugly as the one she had derided. This event naturally distresses her, and she wonders what her husband will say. She orders her women to have the child drowned; but they report the affair to the King instead. Floridas says: "Puis quil a pleu a Dieu me lenuoyer: il le me fault prendre en patience." He orders it baptized, but will not see it. Young Theseus grows fast—and ugly.

A courtier named Fernagus falls in love with the Queen. He speaks to her, but she bids him hold his peace, on pain of her divulging everything. Prompted now by fear of her, Fernagus tells the King that Theseus is really the son of Corvitant the dwarf.[13] The King believes the tale; so do the barons. They agree that she should be burnt. A faithful knight hurries out to warn her. (Here the MS. begins.) She flees. Her disappearance is taken as an admission of guilt. Floridas now orders the death of his young son:

> fol. 5b   Faictes que theseus ait la vie finnee;
> Jamais de coste moy ne dormira journee,
> Je ne vueil point nourir filz de pute afolee.

So Theseus is led out into the forest near Cologne to be put to death. From the squires who conduct him he learns of the accusation of bastardy. He responds by mighty blows which evoke pain and admiration in the squires. They think it a pity that so gallant a spirit should be lodged in such a body. They tell him he must die. He suddenly becomes gentle and prays for the father who has wronged him. A miracle now occurs.[14] The boy becomes as beautiful and strong as his heredity would properly make him. He returns to Cologne with the amazed squires.

Floridas is still seeking his wife, who has taken refuge with a discreet knight named Geoffrey. The dwarf is brought in and given a chance to protest his innocence, and to offer combat, in spite of his diminutive stature. The barons begin to smile and to speak in his behalf. Floridas hesitates. At this moment the transformed Theseus appears. He demands that the accused Queen his mother be brought forth. He says, "King of Cologne, do you not know me? I have little cause to love you, for you have denied me without reason and decreed my death;

---

[12] Folk-Book, fol. 1b.
[13] On fol. 11a of the MS., the dwarf's name is given as Luras.
[14] Cf. a similar situation in *The King of Tars,* ed. K. Breul, Oppeln, 1886, 1895.

know of a truth that I hold it unfitting to call you my father until you have brought back my mother, who is innocent of the grievous charge put upon her." Floridas asks in delight and doubt whether this is really his son. The squires assure him that it is. They tell of the miracle they witnessed. The King expresses regret for his behavior towards his son, who sagely replies:

> fol. 10a   Vous mauez engendre par droit engendrement . . .
> Si pouez bien sur moy mo*n*strer vo maltalent;
> Mais vo*us* auez mespris trop grandement,
> Cest a douter ma mere[15] tant jay le cuer dolent.

The King embraces him again after this wise speech. The Queen is led forth by the faithful Geoffrey. Fernagus would like to escape, but neither bystanders nor readers wish to be cheated of the picturesque combat of the villain (under handicap) with the dwarf. Of course the just side triumphs and wickedness is punished.

5. *Hirlanda of Brittany*, folk-book in the British Museum: *Hirlanda, die gekrönte Unschuld*, ca. 1700. Title-page missing.

This edition begins with a moral discourse of 180 pages in an exceedingly flamboyant style. At last the author approaches the story of his heroine. Hirlanda's husband, Artus of Brittany, departs for war, leaving her with a moral speech of farewell. While Hirlanda remains at home waiting for the birth of her child, Gerard, her brother-in-law, is working against both of them in England. He is anxious to destroy his nephew and become his brother's successor. So, when the sick King of England learns that he can be cured only by the blood and heart of a new-born child, "gantz warm und rohe/ wie es auss dem Leib genommen," Gerard agrees to obtain them. He crosses to Brittany, bribes Hirlanda's nurses, and smuggles the child out of the country. But the child is captured by armed men and later rescued by a prelate.

When Hirlanda asks to see her child, they tell her that it was a shapeless monster, "ein rohes Stuck Fleisch," which they have already buried. Gerard circulates the tale that she had killed the child because it was a bastard. Hirlanda flees, for she hears that her husband has given orders for her death.

Artus returns to an empty house. Seven years later, a nobleman of his, Olive, discovers Hirlanda tending flocks in the guise of a peasant woman. Artus takes her back, rather against her will. "Hat nit Gerard," she says to Olive, "noch den alten Antrib mir zu schaden/ und sein Bruder die vorige Unbesonnenheit zu glauben/ ohne Verhorung dess anderen Theils?"[16] Artus had thought she was dead, yet he receives her with apologies for what she has suffered. At the end of seven years, Hirlanda bears a second child, again to the annoyance of Gerard. "Gerard

---

[15] MS., *cest a ma douter mere*.   [16] P. 280.

der Bösswicht/ als er sahe dass ihme durch die Geburt diser Erbin/ der Zuspruch auff seines Bruders Erbschafft auss Handen gienge/ fasste das verfluchte Vorhaben/ ihme den Ursprung solcher neuen Frucht verdächtig zu machen." [17] He bribes a nobleman to accuse Hirlanda of unfaithfulness with Olive, and she is promptly condemned to the stake. But the first child, enlightened by an angelic vision of his guardian, appears in time to rescue his mother and completely clear her name.

6. *Theseus de Cologne:* the story of Theseus and Flore, or The Golden Eagle. MS., fol. 16b-161a; folk-book, 17a-139b.—Theseus leaves his reconciled mother and father (see summary 4) to search for adventure. He arrives in Rome and lodges with a goldsmith. Here he sees a likeness of the Princess of Rome, Flore, whose father guards her strictly, refusing her to all. This jealous parent is none other than Esmere, the successful young hero of *Florence de Rome,* now grown old and become a typical Danaë's father.[18] Theseus resolves to gain this difficult beauty for himself. He disguises himself as a messenger and demands her in his own name from the Emperor. He is rebuffed:

> fol. 22b Telz xl plus grant ma fille ont demandee
> Qui ne lont point eue ne laront de lannee.
> Sire dit theseus or layes bien gardee,
> Si vous ne lui donnes par la vertue louee,
> En la fin vous porra bien estre emblee.

With this veiled threat he leaves. He persuades the goldsmith to hide him in a large golden eagle, which is transported as a gift to the chamber of Flore. When Theseus first reveals himself to her, she is overcome with fright; but his second attempt is so far successful that he rapidly wins his way to her heart. His pleading and his assurances that he is of noble descent move her to arrange a secret marriage. Meantime the powerful heathen Abilant of Constantinople has demanded her in marriage, and her father has replied, in his obstinate ignorance,

> fol. 36a Dictes a vo sire qui gresse doit garder
> Que je nay nulle fille que ly doye donner,
> Ne ma fille si na talent de marier.

Within a few days Theseus and Flore have made their escape, but they soon encounter disaster. They are captured and violently separated by the heathen forces under Abilant. Theseus is carried off to Antioch. Of course, all available heathen princes fall in love with Flore. Abilant marries her, but is immediately killed by a rival. Flore is taken to Constantinople, where the people hail her as Empress. They also receive her child as their Emperor's heir and successor, though the boy is really the son of Theseus.

[17] P. 315.

[18] His appearance here is an indication of the lateness of *Theseus de Cologne.*

Griffon, the Emperor's brother, is very much annoyed at the birth of the child. He had hoped to succeed to the throne himself. He orders the infant's death, but a passing knight rescues him from the assassins and rears him under the name Gadifer. He has heard the current version of the boy's ancestry, and believes that he is harboring Abilant's son.

Everyone in the story is now "triste et dolent." Esmere wages war on Cologne in revenge for the stealing of his daughter. Griffon wishes to return her to her father, and she is sent back in spite of her terrified protestations that he will surely put her to death. Esmere angrily orders her into prison. He also holds captive the parents of Theseus, who have succumbed to his greater power. The war continues. Theseus appears from distant parts to rescue his parents, his wife, and his city from the grasp of his fanatically hostile father-in-law. Cologne is besieged once more. Combats and sieges are prolonged endlessly.

Gadifer, son of Theseus, grows up. When he learns the story of his supposed ancestry he has already married his foster sister Osanne. He goes to Constantinople to revenge himself on the traitor Griffon, and to claim the city as his heritage. He succeeds. But Griffon summons many allies to help him, including Theseus (who is at peace with his father-in-law at last). Thus it comes about that young Gadifer captures his own father in battle, and hears the true tale of his birth by cross-examination of his distinguished prisoner afterwards. A few wars remain to be settled, and then the way is clear to a conclusion through a series of reconciliations.

7. *Seghelijn van Jerusalem.* The author of this poem is unknown, but there is evidence that he wrote in Flanders, ca. 1330-1350, not long after Jacob van Maerlant's death.[19] The poem as a whole seems original, though it is heavily indebted to French romance for individual episodes (such as the Crescentia-adventures of Seghelijn's wife). The MS. is, like that of *Esmoreit,* a paper codex of the early fifteenth century. There are a number of early prints.[20]

The poem has been discussed from time to time since 1856, but usually as philological material only. Little attention has been given to origins and analogues of the plot. The similarity of the story to *Crescentia,* the Grail romances, *Oedipus,*[21] and the whole family of beprophesied children has also been neglected. The method of exposure because of prophecy here forms an interesting parallel to *Esmoreit.*—

The King of Jerusalem and his wife Blensefleur are expecting a child.

---

[19] Ed. J. Verdam, Leiden, 1878, vi.

[20] Antwerp, 1511; Antwerp, 1517; one as early as 1484, perhaps (see Campbell, *Annales de la Typographie Néerlandaise,* The Hague, 1874, no. 980). An edition before 1517, omitted from Petit's Bibliography, is contained in the Leiden University Library. Verdam mentions all of these in his introduction.

[21] W. Benary, ZfRP, XXXVII, 622, called attention to the relation of *Seghelijn* to the cycle of Gregorios and the Emperor Constant.

The King summons the court astrologer, who prophesies that the boy will kill his father-in-law and become a Christian. The King immediately resolves to struggle against fate by ordering his son's death. But when he tells the Queen, she resolves with equal firmness to save the child. She shows great courage in achieving her purpose. She goes out alone into the forest to bear her child, to save it from its father. Three "prophetesses of God" give the child three gifts: *seghe* (victory), irresistible eyes, and the promise of heaven after his death. They take the infant, and bid its mother substitute a stillborn child. Seghelijn is given to a fisherman to be reared. The King is deceived, and rejoices in his supposed security; but the astronomer tells him that his child is living nevertheless. The King seeks his wife and questions her. She asks him if he is mad. He leaves her room, finds the astrologer outside, and simply kills him.[22]

When Seghelijn has grown sufficiently, he is sent to the city with fish. The Queen notices him, and gives him gold so that he may go back to school. His foster father takes it away from him. The next time Seghelijn receives bounty, he tells his foster father that he got it by killing a man. He is greeted then by the inevitable taunt *vondelinc*, and he demands to know the truth. When he hears the tale and receives the ring left with him by the prophetesses, he resolves to seek his parents. As weapon, he receives a rusty sword, formerly used by St. Peter to cut off the soldier's ear. When he appears before the Queen again, his ring leads to recognition; but she asks him to keep his identity secret from his father. This he agrees to do. He preaches Christianity to her.

His position at court evokes envy, especially from Robbolijn, a conventional *chanson de geste* villain. This false knight inflames the King against him on several pretexts. It comes to a fight in which the King takes part against Seghelijn; but the latter, knowing the prophecy, determines not to be a parricide, and he behaves with great forbearance. The King is touched. But now Robbolijn whispers that the Queen and Seghelijn love each other, for he has noticed the young man change color when she says, "Willecome, lieve kint!" Seghelijn resolves to break away from this entangling net of jealousy. His mother embraces him. Robbolijn sees and reports this scene. He accuses Seghelijn openly, and is killed for his pains. The King is helpless to resent this, so long as he sees his son's irresistible eyes. That night an angel warns Seghelijn to flee.

The young man departs after a sorrowful farewell from his mother. He goes through many adventures which are described with great zest and animation. One, at the castle of his maternal uncle, is an obvious imitation of the traditional Grail scene.[23] In another adventure, he becomes the father of the Seven Sages of Rome. Then he marries Flor-

---

[22] The abrupt exit of the astrologer removes one of the strongest similarities to *Esmoreit*.   [23] P. 43.

ette, daughter of St. Helena, whose sufferings have already been described. The prophecy is fulfilled as in the story of St. Julian. Seghelijn's father comes to Rome, with Blensefleur, to be cured of a disease. Florette receives them in her husband's absence. When she learns who they are, she treats them with great honor and surrenders her room to them. A traitor tells Seghelijn that his wife has a lover with her. Seghelijn rushes to the room without removing his spurs, and kills his sleeping parents. An angel reveals what he has done. Florette comes in. He drops his sword and tells her, horrified. She dies on the spot. Seghelijn retires to a forest and does penance for fifty years, at the end of which time—like Gregorius der guote Sundaere—he is chosen Pope.

8. *Charles le Chauve*, MS. Bibl. Nat. 24,372. The story of Dieudonné begins on folio 22a. His father Phillip, son of Charles le Chauve, after winning a wife and kingdom for himself in Sicily, departs for Jerusalem before the birth of his son. He leaves Butor in charge of Queen Dorame. This false seneschal, like so many others, tries to win her for himself, first by reporting her husband's death, then by arguments, and finally by force; but she, like many other virtuous queens, responds by knocking out three of his teeth. He thereupon bribes the *sage-femme* by a promise of marriage and the royal crown to destroy the child who would stand in the way of both of them. When Dieudonné is born and the Queen is lying asleep,

> fol. 23a Celle vint a sa dame *et* son enfant li prent
> Et li mist .1. poulet estranle laidement.

The child is given over to Butor, who orders a varlet to have it killed. When the man is about to murder it, his heart is moved in the conventional way by the sight of the infant's smile. He exposes Dieudonné on the branch of a tree, where a passing knight finds him. He takes him home to be reared with his son and daughter.

When the barons come to take their young prince to be baptised, the false nurse discloses the chicken and cries:

> fol. 24a Ay fausce royne vo corps soit maleis
> Mengie aves lenfant car du sanc *est* honnis
> Li viaire de v*ous et* trestous en rougis.

Butor feigns great horror:

> fol. 24a Butor tout en criant cest du lieu dep*ar*tis
> En le salle est ven*us* si trouua les marchis
> A haute vois leur crie seigneurs po*ur* ih*es*u cris
> Que ferons de no dame do*nt* li corps soit honnis
> Elle ne weult me*n*gier que*n*fancho*ns* petis.

The Queen protests, and tells the story of his behavior to her:

> fol. 24a Lautre jour me requist li glous de druerie
> Et me dist *que* mort *est* li sires de hongrie.[24]

Butor consents to have her imprisoned, instead of being burnt at once.

During the childhood of Dieudonné as a foundling, he is often taunted by his foster brother who is jealous of him; but his foster sister is loyal to him. She falls in love with him and asks him to marry her when they are grown up. But her brother quarrels violently with Dieudonné, who is forced to kill him in self-defense. The foundling thereupon departs to find his parents, as he had long since resolved to do. After some adventures he arrives at the castle of a fairy named Gloriande, who tells him about his parentage and exposure. Thence he proceeds to the rescue of his mother, as do so many other foundlings in medieval fiction.

[24] *Hongrie* is often used to designate the kingdom of Sicily in this romance. The author seems to know the island well. His high regard for it is expressed fol. 7a.

APPENDIX III

CHAUCER, GOWER, AND TRIVET

The question of the relationship of Chaucer and Gower to Trivet and to each other has been discussed several times since the publication of Trivet's chronicle. Before that time, Tyrwhitt naturally supposed that Chaucer's only source was Gower; and later, Wright (ed. of Canterbury Tales, I, 206) and Furnivall (note to Brock's ed. of Trivet for the Chaucer Society) thought that Chaucer drew on a lost French romance, while Gower had used Trivet. In 1892, Lücke (*Anglia* XIV, 77-112 and 149-185) made a careful comparison of the three versions, in great detail, and proved conclusively that Chaucer also used Trivet directly, since many details omitted or changed by Gower are identical in Chaucer and Trivet. Lücke infers from this that Chaucer used both Gower and Trivet; but there is nothing in his evidence to prove that it was not Gower who used both Chaucer and Trivet. Lücke does not state why he thinks Gower wrote first.

Tatlock considers this matter in some detail (*Development and Chronology*, p. 172 ff.). He is convinced that Chaucer must have written after the completion of Gower's *Confessio Amantis* for several reasons. In the first place, the Introduction to the *Man of Law's Prologue*, which expresses horror at the wicked example of Canace and Apollonius of Tyre (both incest-stories), is supposed to refer to Gower's treatment of them in the *Confessio*.[1] It may be replied that the words of the Man of Law are just as much a condemnation of Ovid, Gower's source for Canace's story, as they are of Gower himself; and since Chaucer no doubt knew other treatments of Apollonius than that in the *Confessio*, it is not necessary to suppose that Gower had as yet written these tales when the *Man of Law's Tale* was composed. There is another reason why these remarks may have been prefixed to the story of Constance without any reference to Gower's work. It is hardly possible that Chaucer did not know some of the many medieval versions, like *Emare*, in which the heroine is driven into exile by an incestuous father, and the assurance that "Chaucer" does not treat of such "unkinde abhominaciouns" may simply mark his deliberate choice of a version which—no matter how awkwardly—does away with them. One trait in the story itself, as told by all three writers, preserves a trace of the Incestuous Father plot. When Constance arrives in England, according to Trivet, "entre ses ditz riens ne voleit reconustre de Tiberie, lemperour, son piere, ne del soudan." Chaucer says

[1] Root, *The Poetry of Chaucer*, rejects this argument.

> 524 But what she was, she wolde no man seye,
> For foul ne fair, thogh that she shulde deye.

When she arrives in Rome, where her father is, both Gower and Chaucer emphasize her reticence and her aversion to telling anything about herself. This seems strange, since she has no reason to suppose that her father would not welcome her with open arms. Tatlock (p. 180, n.) suggests that she is really an other-world character who may not reveal her name; but is it not more likely that the silence of Constance is due to versions like *Emare* and *La Manekine*, in which the heroine has excellent reasons for concealing her whereabouts? Probably Chaucer, Gower, and Trivet had such tales in mind as they wrote. Possibly these tales suggested the exclamation of the Man of Law against incest-stories in general.

Another argument used to establish Gower's precedence is Chaucer's comment concerning the invitation sent to the Emperor at the end by Constance and Alla:

> 1086 Som men wold seyn, how that the child Maurice
> Doth this message un-to the emperour,

but Chaucer believes that Alla had more sense of the fitness of things than to send a child. Tatlock argues that "Som men" must mean Gower, because, although Trivet says the same thing about Maurice, few people would be likely to have read the Anglo-Norman chronicle in comparison with those who had read the *Confessio Amantis*. This is plausible, but the fact remains that Chaucer *could* have found the incident in Trivet alone.

Arguments based on style and verse-form have been advanced to prove that the *Man of Law's Tale* is early work: Skeat thinks that it antedates the *Confessio*, at least in its first form, and was revised for the *Canterbury Tales*; Pollard agrees that the date is early. The use of rime royal has been thought to indicate composition before the *Canterbury Tales*. These are matters of subjective judgment; but it does not seem at all impossible to me that Chaucer chose to return to the stanzaic form in telling a story which he thought fitting to that style of expression; nor do I see traces of youthful inexperience in the telling of it. The plot is weak, repetitious, and diffuse, of course; but so are most plots of accused queens. Chaucer was hardly the one to change the general plan of a story which was known in so many treatments: he contented himself with the choice of a version in which the most unpleasing feature had been removed.

As Tatlock says, there seems to be no presumption one way or the other, since the similarities between Gower and Chaucer in wording (some of them are very close) might have resulted from borrowing by either from either. In general, the evidence of the lateness of the *Man of*

Law's Tale[2] strengthens the likelihood that Gower wrote first and Chaucer used him. Chaucer agrees with Gower wherever the latter deviates noticeably from Trivet (except for the worse deviations); and Gower, who was not noted for condensation, omits Chaucer's elaborations such as the description of Constance. The balance seems to be in favor of Gower's priority, though none of the evidence is conclusive.

One important deviation of Gower from Trivet and Chaucer concerns the attitude of the Sultaness to Constance. The latter two account for the hatred of the old Queen because of the obligation to change her religion, but Gower says:

> 639 But that which nevere was wel herted,
> Envie tho began travaile
> In disturbance of this spousaile . . .

The Sultaness reflects

> 626   If so it is
> Mi sone him wedde in this manere,
> Than have I lost my joies hiere,
> For myn astat schal so be lassed.

This change in motive, which Gower carries out consistently, brings his story closer to märchen and romances about queens accused by a jealous mother-in-law, whose motive is, as we have seen, resentment at the loss of honor and dignity to a younger woman. The reason for the change is of course Gower's general plan, in which each tale illustrates a sin against love; and the story of Constance is very easily adapted, by this slight modification, to the purpose of illustrating envy. In making the change—which seems like a reversion to type—Gower may have been influenced by the numerous cycles like *Octavian* and the *Swan Children*, which contain envious mothers-in-law. When he treats of the second persecution, by Domild, he does not give a motive (Chaucer and Trivet say that Constance was "hated" by Alla's mother as a "stranger" whom the people loved), but one infers the same sin: envy. If Chaucer, in comparing Gower with Trivet, was faced with the necessity of choosing between their accounts of the behavior of the Sultaness, he would have no reason for deviating from the older text of Trivet, since he was not following any scheme like that of the *Confessio Amantis*.[3] The treatment of this episode by Chaucer is perhaps a piece of evidence in favor of Lücke's thesis that he used both Gower and Trivet.

---

[2] The failure of Alcestis to mention this tale of feminine constancy in the prologue to the *Legend of Good Women*; the inclusion of passages from Innocent's *De Contemptu Mundi*, the translation of which seems to have been a comparatively late work of Chaucer.

[3] This reversion of Chaucer to Trivet —if it be a reversion—weakens Tupper's argument that the *Canterbury Tales* were intended to illustrate the seven deadly sins. If the *Tale of Constance* is supposed to illustrate envy as in Gower, Chaucer might have emphasized his point as Gower did; but I think it is precisely because he is *not* telling the story as an example of envy that he uses Trivet's motivation without change.

INDEX

INDEX

Adonis: 40.
Agapios of Crete: 31 n.
Aiol: 104 n., 117.
Albericus Trium Fontium: 104, 105.
Albert of Bonstetten: *Life of St. Idda,* 108 n.
Alixandre, Roy de Hongrie: 69 n., 71.
Amadis of Gaul: 117.
Amis and Amiles: 92 n.
Amor and Psyche: 34, 54.
Ancona, A. d': *Sacre Rappresentazioni,* 69 n.
Animal birth: accusation of, 11, 21-37, 39, 46, 47, 53, 60, 61, 62, 63, 64, 76 ff., 113; belief in, 22.
Apollodorus: *Epitome,* 45 and n.
Apollonius of Tyre: 75 n., 132.
Arabian Nights: 29 n., 48, 109.
Arfert, P.: *Das Motiv von der unterschobenen Braut,* 54 n.
Aron, A. W.: *Matriarchy in Germanic Hero-Lore,* 34 n., 43 n.
Atalanta: 45.
Avenstrup and Treitel: *Isländische Märchen,* 33, 58.
Ayres, H. M.: Tr. of *Esmoreit,* 10 n.

Bäckström: *Svenska Folkböcker,* 5, 111 n.
Banished Wife's Lament: 109.
Baudoin de Sebourc: 100 n., 117, 118, 119.
Beatrix: 81.
Beaumanoir: 5 n., 69.
Bédollierre, M. E.: Ed. *Genevieve of Brabant,* 106 n.
Belle Hélène de Constantinople, La: 5, 29, 64, 69 n., 70 f., 74, 76, 78, 119, 120-121.
Benary, W.: 128 n.
Beowulf: 65 n., 67, 68.
Berg, L. P. C. van den: *Nederlandsche Volksromanen,* 82 n.
Berta, daughter of Charlemagne: 67.
Bey, G. Spitta: 49 n.
Birck, Johannes: *Chronicle,* 111.
Blade, J. F.: *Contes Recueillis en Armagnac,* 29 n.
Blöde, J. F. D.: *Der historische Schwanritter,* 78 n.
Boer, R. C.: on the Offa-story, 67 n.
Boeve de Hamptone: 117, 118.

Bolte and Polívka: *Anmerkungen zu den Märchen der Brüder Grimm,* 23, 24 n., 49 and n.
Botermans, A. J.: *Die seven wijse Mannen van Romen,* 79 n.
Brandt, C. J.: *Romantisk Digting fra Middelalderen,* 99 n.
Breul, K.: Ed. *The King of Tars,* 125.
Bruce, J. D.: Ed. *Historia Meriadoci,* 117 n.
Brugmann: see Leskien and Brugmann.
Büheler: *Königstochter von Frankreich,* 64, 69 n., 73.
Burton: *Supplemental Arabian Nights,* 48 n.

Caesar de Nostradamus: *Chronicle,* 99 n.
Callaway, Henry: *Nursery Tales of the Zulus,* 22 n.
Campbell, J. F.: *Popular Tales of the West Highlands,* 38 n.
Campbell, Killis: *The Seven Sages of Rome,* 79.
Campbell, M. F. A. G.: 128 n.
Canace: 132.
Canterbury Tales: 3.
Carnoy, H.: *Lit. Orale de la Picardie,* 15, 16.
Cerisiers, René de: *Genevieve de Brabant,* 106 n.
Chambers, R. W.: *Introd. to the Study of Beowulf,* 65, 68.
Chansons de geste: 11, 82, 93, 95, 100, 101, 104, 112, 114, 129.
Charlemagne-cycle: 98.
Charles le Chauve: 102, 118, 119, 130-131.
Chaucer: 3, 5, 6, 7, 8, 11, 13, 21, 23, 24, 61, 63, 64, 70, 74 n., 75, 77, 78, 100, 104 n., 110, 114, 132-134.
Chevalier au Cygne: 6, 81, 94.
Chrétien de Troyes: 3.
Cinderella: 24, 36 and n., 37 ff., 44, 64, 65, 70 n.
Cinyras: 40.
Circourt, de: Ed. *Le Victorial,* 70 n.
Clouston, W. A.: 49 n.
Clymenus: 40.
Columpnarium: 70 n., 73.
Comtesse d'Anjou, La: 69 n., 71, 76.
Confessio Amantis: 132 ff.

Constance-story: 3, 4, 5, 9, 11, 13, 23, 26, 61, 62, 63, 64 n., 67, 74 and n., 75 n., 84, 88, 91, 100, 104 n., 110, 114; analogues of, 5, 7, 8, 132 ff.; sources of, 5, 6.
Copland's *Knight of the Swan:* 84.
Corington, R. H.: *The Melanesians,* 18.
Cosquin, Emmanuel: *Contes Populaires de Lorraine,* 38 n., 50.
Co-wife as persecutor: 14, 20, 21, 23, 26, 46, 49.
Cox, Marion R.: *Cinderella,* 36 n., 70.
Crane, T. F.: *Italian Popular Tales,* 50.
Crescentia-story: 39, 75 n., 108, 109 ff., 128.
Crooke, W.: *Popular Religion of Northern India,* 17.
Curr, E.: *The Australian Race,* 17.
Curtin, J.: *Folktales of the Russians,* 57.
Cyneþryð: 68.
Cyrus the Great: 56 n.

Damiet: 34, 117, 119.
Damietta: 118 f.
Danaë: 56, 58, 59, 117, 127.
Danish ballads: 96 n.
Däumling, H.: *Das Mädchen ohne Hände,* 26 n., 36 n., 69 n.
Dirr, A.: *Kaukasische Märchen,* 16, 50.
Dit de Florence de Rome, Le: 111.
Dit de l'Empereur Constant, Le: 26, 117, 128 n.
Dolopathos: 79, 80, 119.
Donegild: 4, 5, 6, 24, 77, 114.
Doon de la Roche: 95 f., 119, 123-124.
Doon de Maience: 102, 117.
Dozon, Auguste: *Contes Albanais,* 38 n., 50.
Drida: 67.

Ellis, W.: *Polynesian Researches,* 18.
Emare: 6, 69 n., 70 n., 71, 74, 76 n., 77, 132, 133.
Emmich, Matthias: *Genevieve of Brabant,* 106 n.
Enfances Garin de Montglane: 119.
Enikel, Jansen: *Weltchronik,* 69 n., 73.
Enrrique Fi de Oliva: 95 n.
Envious sister as persecutor: 23, 47 ff., 53, 79.
Epopeus of Lesbos: 40.
Erechtheus: 40.
Erl of Toulouse: 99, 103.
Esmoreit: 9 ff., 34, 54, 56, 91 n., 96, 100, 107, 113, 114, 117 ff., 128, 129.

Exchanged Letter story: 5, 11, 23-37, 44, 46, 47, 52, 53, 64 ff., 76 ff., 82, 83.
Exposed children: 14, 114.
Eyre, E. J.: *Expeditions of Discovery into Central Australia,* 18 n.

Fabliaux: 3.
Fabula Romanensis: 69 n.
Falentins og Ursins Saga: 94 n.
Fallersleben, Hoffmann von: 9 n.
Farnsworth, W. O.: *Uncle and Nephew in the Chansons de Geste,* 34 n.
Father as persecutor: 29, 31, 32, 46, 56, 113.
Father-in-law as persecutor: 10, 33, 45, 56, 60, 117.
Fazio, Bartolomeo: 69 n., 73, 77, 78.
Figlia del Re di Dacia, La: 69 n., 71.
Fiorentino, Giovanni: *Il Pecorone,* 69 n.
Fleury, Jean: *Lit. Orale de la Basse-Normandie,* 27.
Florence de Rome: 6, 7 and n., 109 n., 110 and n., 111, 127.
Florent et Lyon: 86 n.
Florent et Octavian: 86, 87, 92.
Florentina de Getrouwe: 120.
Floriant et Florete: 117, 119.
Folk-books: 5 n., 9 n., 77 n., 84, 86 n., 88, 89, 93, 99, 104 n., 105 and n., 107, 109 n., 117, 118, 122 n.
Folk-lore (of accused queens): 7 ff.
Forcheur, Florian: *La Belle Hélène de Constantinople,* 120.
Frazer, Sir J. G.: *The Golden Bough,* 17, 19 n., 40, 41, 42; *Totemism and Exogamy,* 18, 19 n., 43 n., 44 n.
Freher, Marquard: *Origines Palatinae,* 106 n.
Fritzlar, Herman von: 74 n.

Galerent: 81.
Galland: Translator of *Arabian Nights,* 48 n.
Gamez, Diaz de: *Le Victorial,* 70 n.
Ganelon: 95, 96, 101, 104 and n., 114, 123.
Gautier de Coinsi: 110 n.
Genevieve of Brabant: 99 n., 104 n., 106, 107, 108, 119.
Gesta Romanorum: 104 n., 111.
Gidel, Ch.: *Études sur la Lit. Grecque Moderne,* 31 n.
Gloriant: 117.
Golden Eagle, The: 127.
Golz, B.: *Pfalzgräfin Genoveva,* 106 n.

INDEX

Gonzenbach, Laura: *Sicilianische Märchen*, 27 n., 37 n., 50, 56, 57, 58 n.
Gough: *On the Constance-Saga*, 6, 64, 70 n.; Ed. *Emare*, 69 n.
Gower, John: 70, 74 n., 75, 132-134.
Grail-story: 128, 129.
Gran Conquista de Ultramar: 82, 104 n.
Grässe, J. G. T.: Ed. *Gesta Romanorum*, 111 n.
Gregorius-legend: 51 n., 128 n., 130.
Grimm: *Märchen*, 28, 29 n., 33, 36, 49 n., 78 n., 79, 80, 81; *Deutsche Sagen*, 82 n.
Griseldis: 120.
Groot, J. J. M. de: *Religious System of China*, 17.
Grundtvig, Svend: 97, 98.
Gubernatis, A. de: *Tradizioni Popolari*, 24, 33, 37 n., 50.
Guessard, M. F.: Ed. *Macaire*, 104 n.
Guglielma, Saint: 110 n.
Guillaume de Palerne: 117, 118.
Guinevere, 101 n.

Hagen, H. von der: *Crescentia*, 109 n., 111; *Künigin von Frankrich*, 104 n.; *Schwanensage, Die*, 78 n.
Hahn, J. G. von: *Griechische Märchen*, 16 and n., 39 n., 50, 55 n., 58.
Hambruch, Paul: *Malaiische Märchen*, 22 n., 55 n.; *Südseemärchen*, 33 n.
Harpalyce: 40.
Hartland, E. S.: *Legend of Perseus*, 59 n.; *Primitive Society*, 41 n., 42, 43 n., 44 and n., 46, 53.
Heiligenleben, Das: 78.
Heinzel, R.: *Über die ostgothische Heldensage*, 101 and n., 104.
Helena Antonia of Constantinopel: 5.
Helena, Saint: 77 n., 130.
Helyas, Knight of the Swan: 81, 94.
Henry of Huntington: 39 n.
Henry the Fowler: 38, 39, 67.
Herbert le Clerc: 79 n.
Herodotus: 56 n.
Herzog Herpin: 69 n., 73 n., 117. (See also *Lion de Bourges*.)
Hildegard-story: 109, 111.
Hilka, Alfons: Ed. *Dolopathos*, 79 n.
Hippeau, C.: Ed. *Chevalier au Cygne*, 81 n.
Hippodamia: 45.
Hirlanda of Brittany: 7, 106, 107 and n., 108, 126.

Historia del Rey de Hungria: 69 n., 71.
Historia Meriadoci: 117.
Hocleve, Thomas: *Fabula de Quadam Imperatrice*, 111.
Hollis, A. C.: *The Masai*, 14 n.
Holthausen, F.: Ed. *Beowulf*, 65.
Howitt, A. W.: *Native Tribes of South East Australia*, 18.
Huet, B.: *La Légende du Chevalier au Cygne*, 79 and n.
Hugdietrich: 100, 101 n., 117.
Huon de Bordeaux: 69 n.
Hyginus: 24, 40 and n.

Idda of Tockenburg: 7, 106, 107, 108.
Imbriani, V.: *La Novellaja Fiorentina*, 33, 48, 50.
Incestuous Father as persecutor: 5, 24, 35 ff., 43, 44, 45, 46, 52, 56, 64 ff., 132.
Infanticide: as accusation, 11, 39, 49, 52, 60, 90, 91, 102 n., 107, 113; causes of, 19; for sacrifice, 19 ff.
Infidelity, accusation of: 29 n., 30, 31, 32, 46, 53, 61, 63, 81, 83, 88, 95, 107, 113.
Innocent III: *De Contemptu Mundi*, 132 n.
Ipomedon: 119.
Isomberte: 82.

Jacques d'Acqui: 77 n.
Jan uut den Vergiere: 9 n., 118, 119.
Jealous husband as persecutor: 46, 60 f., 62, 96, 117.
Jecklin, Dietrich: *Volkstümliches aus Graubünden*, 28 n.
Johannes de Alta Silva: 79, 81.
Jourdains de Blaivies: 75 n., 117, 119.
Jubinal, A.: *Nouveau Recueil des Contes*, 111 n.
Julian, Saint: 130.

Kaakebeen and Ligthard: Ed. *Esmoreit*, 9 n.
Kaiserchronik: 109 n.
Kalff, G.: *Middelnederlandsche epische Fragmenten*, 89 n., 91 n.
Karadschitsch, W. S.: *Volksmärchen der Serben*, 31 n.
Karlamagnus Saga: 95 n.
Karlmeinet: 98.
Keller, Adelbert von: Ed. *Karlmeinet*, 98 n.
Kempten, Abbey of: 111.
King of Tars, The: 125 n.

140 CHAUCER'S CONSTANCE AND ACCUSED QUEENS

Klemming, G. E.: *Namnlös och Valentin*, 91 n.
Knust, Hermann: *Italienische Märchen*, 25 n.
Koch, J.: *Der gegenwärtige Stand der Chaucer-Forschung*, 6.
Köhler, R.: 109 n., 117 n.
Koningin Sibille: 104 n.
Krauss, F. S.: *Sagen und Märchen der Südslaven*, 57.
Kretschmer, P.: *Neugriechische Märchen*, 50.
Kühn and Schwartz: *Norddeutsche Sagen*, 20, 38 n., 81 n.
Künigin von Frankrîch, Die, 104.
Kúnos, I.: *Türkische Volksmärchen*, 21 n., 25 n., 50.
Kydske Dronning, Den: 99.

Landres-þattr: 95 n., 97, 98.
Lawrence, W. W.: 109 n.
Lay of the Ash: 81.
Leendertz, P.: *Middelnederlandsche dramatische Poezie*, 9 n.
Legrand, Emile: *Recueil de Contes Grecs*, 30 n., 38 n., 50.
Leskien, A.: *Balkanmärchen*, 38 n., 50.
Leskien and Brugmann: *Litauische Märchen*, 36 n.
Life-tokens: 53.
Ligthard: see Kaakebeen and Ligthard.
Lion de Bourges: 69 n., 104 n., 119.
Livre de Baudoyn, Le: 118 and n., 119.
Louis, Saint: 118.
Lowie, Robert H.: *Primitive Society*, 34 n.
Löwis of Menar, A. von: *Finnische Märchen*, 12 n.; *Russische Märchen*, 15, 32 n., 39 n.
Lücke, E.: *Trivet, Gower und Chaucer*, 74 n., 132, 134.
Lüdthe, Gustav: Ed. *Erl of Toulouse*, 99 n.
Luzel, F. M.: *Légendes Chrétiennes*, 31 n., 47 n., 58.

Mabinogion: 94 n.
Macaire: 93, 104 f., 111 n., 113, 114.
Madden, Sir F.: Ed. *Gesta Romanorum*, 111 n.
Maerlant, Jacob van: 128.
Mai und Beaflor: 36, 69, 71, 74, 77.
Maillart, Jehan: 69 n.
Malegijs: 91 n., 93 n., 117, 118, 119.
Man of Law's Tale: see Constance-story.

Manekine, La: 5 n., 45 n., 46, 69 n., 71 n., 72, 73, 74, 75 n., 77, 133.
Massmann, H. F.: Ed. *Kaiserchronik*, 109 n.
Matabrune: 6, 81, 82, 83, 88, 114.
Matriarchy: 33 f., 40 ff., 58, 61; definition of, 41.
Matthew of Paris: 39 n., 65 and n., 66 n.
Maugis d'Aigremont: 93 n., 119.
Meinhof, C.: *Africanische Märchen*, 14 n.
Méon, M.: *Nouveau Recueil de Fabliaux*, 110 n.
Michel, Francisque: see Monmerqué and Michel.
Mijatovies, C.: *Serbian Folk-lore*, 50.
Miracles de Nostre Dame: 69 n., 78.
Mire, Aubert le: *Fasti Belgici*, 104 n.
Mitra, S.: *Sanskrit Buddhist Lit.*, 49 n.
Moltzer, H. E.: *De middelnederlandsche dramatische Poezie*, 9 n.
Monmerqué and Michel: *Théâtre Français du Moyen-Âge*, 82 n.
Moriaen: 119.
Mors, Hella: *Arabische Märchen*, 13 n.
Mort Artu: 101 n.
Mother-in-law as persecutor: 5, 6, 9, 11, 13, 20, 25, 26, 29, 30, 32, 33, 34, 46, 60, 61, 62, 63, 76 ff., 86 ff. 100, 103, 107 n., 113.
Mussafia, A.: 110 n.
Myrrha: 40.

Nachshabī: *Tūtī Nāmeh*, 109.
Naissance du Chevalier au Cygne: 80.
Naumann, H. and I.: *Isländische Märchen*, 38 n., 54 n.
Nennius: 39 n.
Nerucci, Gherardo: *Sessanta Novelle*, 27 n., 29 n., 30 n.
Nijhoff, W.: *Catalogus*, 84 n.
Nyctimene: 40.

Octavian: 86 ff., 91, 93, 94, 96, 99 n., 107, 113, 134.
Oedipus: 18, 117, 128.
Offa: see *Vitae Duorum Offarum*.
Ogier the Dane: 118.
Oliva-story: 95 ff., 101, 119.
Olive, Saint: 29 and n., 35, 69 n., 73, 77.
Oliver and Artus: 92 n.

Palanus: 99.
Paris, Gaston: 80, 98.

INDEX

Paris, P.: *Les Manuscrits Français*, 69 n.
Parise la Duchesse: 6, 7, 100 f., 102, 103, 112, 113, 119.
Pasiphaë: 46 n.
Patriarchy: 41.
Paul the Deacon: 81 n., 99 n.
Pauli, R.: Ed. Gower, 70 n.
Peau d'Âne: 65.
Pecorone, Il: 69 n., 75, 77.
Pentamerone, Il: 76.
Peter, Anton: *Volkstümliches aus Oesterreich-schlesien*, 26 n.
Petit, L.: *Middelnederlandsche Bibliographie*, 105 n., 128.
Plural birth: 81, 83, 88.
Polívka: *see* Bolte and Polívka.
Potter, M. A.: *Sohrab and Rustum*, 53.
Prato, Stanislao: *Quatro Novelline Popolari*, 25 n., 27 n.
Priebsch: 9 n., 118.
Procris: 40.
Pröhle, Heinrich: *Kinder- und Volksmärchen*, 27 n., 50.
Prophecies as cause of persecution: 10, 58, 117, 129.
Prothesileus: 119.
Puckett, H. W.: *The "Genoveva" Theme*, 106 n.
Puymaigre, Count de: *La Fille aux Mains Coupées*, 5, 28; Ed. *Le Victorial*, 70 n.
Pwyll Son of Dyved: 94 n.

Radloff, W.: *Proben der Volkslit. der türkischen Stämme*, 26 n., 30 n., 39.
Reali di Francia: 86, 88.
Regina Stella e Mattabruna, La: 83.
Reiffenberg, Baron de: Ed. *Chevalier au Cygne*, 81.
Reiser, K.: *Sagen des Allgäus*, 111 n.
Rejected lover as accuser: 63, 75, 92, 95 ff., 125.
Remi, Phillipe de: *see* Beaumanoir.
Renier: 118, 119.
Richars li Biaus: 117, 118.
Rickert, Edith: 6, 65 n., 69 n., 70 n., 76 n.
Ridder metter Mouwe, De: 119.
Ritson: *Ancient English Metrical Romances*, 69 n.
Ritter Galmy: 99.
Rivière, J.: *Contes Populaires de la Kabylie du Djurdjura*, 14 n., 21 n.
Robbrecht: 11, 12, 21, 32, 61, 106, 107, 114, 118.
Rohde, Erwin: 75 n.
Roman de la Violette: 6, 75 n.

Romanciero: *Choix de Vieux Chants Portugais*, 36 n.
Root, R. K.: *Poetry of Chaucer*, 132.
Royalle Couronne des Roye d'Arles, La: 99 n.
Ruths, R.: *Die fr. Fassungen der Belle Hélène*, 69 n.

Sandras, E. G.: *Étude sur G. Chaucer*, 6, 7.
Sarrazin, Gregor: Ed. *Octavian*, 86 n.
Sauerland, Ernst: *Ganelon und sein Geschlecht*, 114 n.
Schade, Oskar: Ed. *Crescentia*, 109 n.
Schick, Josef: *Corpus Hamleticum*, 117 n.
Schleicher, August: *Litauische Märchen*, 28 n.
Schmidt, B.: *Griechische Märchen*, 13 n.
Schneller, Christian: *Märchen aus Wälschtirol*, 27 n., 50.
Schott, A. and A.: *Walachische Märchen*, 57.
Sebilla: 104 n.
Sébillot, P.: *Lit. Orale de la Haute Bretagne*, 16, 30 n., 39 n.
Seelmann, W.: *Valentin und Namelos*, 89 n., 91 n., 94 n.
Seghelijn van Jerusalem: 7, 51 n., 75 n., 112, 117, 119, 128 ff.
Seneschal as accuser: *see* Villain as accuser.
Seuffert, B.: *Die Legende von Genovefa*, 106 n.
Seven Sages of Rome, The: 79, 129.
Sicily: 118, 119, 131 n.
Siefken, O.: *Das geduldige Weib*, 6 and n., 75; *Der Konstanze-Griseldistypus*, 6 and n.
Simrock, Karl: *Die deutschen Volksbücher*, 69 n., 99 n.
Sir Degarre: 117.
Sir Eglamour: 117.
Sir Generides: 117.
Sir Tryamour: 104 n., 105.
Sister-in-law as persecutor: 31.
Smyth, R. B.: *Aborigines of Victoria*, 17.
Sohrab and Rustem: 53.
Spencer and Gillen: *Native Tribes of Central Australia*, 18.
Stefanović: 6, 7 n., 39 and n., 66, 109.
Steinberger, Hermann: *Hirlanda von Bretagne*, 107.
Stella: 83.
Stepmother as persecutor: 12, 20, 24, 29, 30, 31, 46, 62, 113.

Stigand, C. H.: *To Abyssinia through an Unknown Land,* 17.
Straparola: 37 n., 38 n.
Streve, Paul: *Die Octavian Sage,* 86 n.
Stroebe, Klara: *Nordische Märchen,* 16 n., 32 n., 57.
Substituted Bride: 54, 60.
Suchier, H.: Ed. of *La Manekine,* 64, 65, 66 n., 69 n., 70 n.
Susannah: 104 and n.
Swan Children story: 62, 78 ff., 87, 91, 93, 106, 107, 113, 122, 134.
Swan Knight: 53, 78 ff.
Sympathetic magic: 53.

Tabu: 54, 60.
Tatlock, J. S. P.: *Development and Chronology of Chaucer's Works,* 132, 133.
Terrebasse, A. de: Ed. *Palanus,* 99.
Theseus de Cologne: 7, 82, 83, 102, 103, 105, 107, 117, 119, 122-123, 125-126, 127-128.
Ðidrekssaga: 103 and n.
Thousand and One Days: 109.
Thousand and One Nights: see Arabian Nights.
Thyestes: 40.
þryð: 68, 75 n.
Todd, H. A.: Ed. *Chevalier au Cygne,* 79, 80 n.
Torrent of Portyngale: 117.
Treason, accusation of: 63, 95, 113.
Treitel: *see* Avenstrup and Treitel.
Tremearne, A. J. M.: *Hansa Superstitions and Customs,* 16 n.
Tristan de Nantueil: 75 n., 119.
Trivet, Nicholas: *Life of Constance,* 5, 64, 70, 74 n., 75 and n., 77, 132-134.
Tupper, F.: 134.
Turias ende Florete: 117.
Tyrwhitt: 132.

Valentine and Nameless: 63, 86, 89 ff., 103, 113, 119.
Valentine and Oursson: 89 ff., 93, 104 n., 113, 119.
Vandelli, G.: Ed. *I Reali di Francia,* 86 n.
Verdam, J.: Ed. *Seghelijn,* 7 n., 112 n., 128 n.

Victorial, Le: 70 n., 72.
Villain as accuser: 11, 15, 32, 61, 63, 94, 95 ff., 107, 108, 113, 117, 123 ff.
Vincent of Beauvais: *Spec. Hist.,* 110 n.
Vitae Duorum Offarum: 5, 39, 64, 65, 66, 67, 74, 75 n., 78.
Vollmöller, Karl: Ed. *Octavian,* 86 n.
Vortigern: 39.
Vreese, W. de: On the Knight of the Swan, 84 n.

Wallensköld, A.: 109, 111 n.
Wardrop, Marjory: *Georgian Fairy Tales,* 57.
Wats, W.: Ed. *Vitae Durorum Offarum,* 65 n.
Wauquelin, Jean: 69 n., 120.
Webster, W.: *Basque Legends,* 39 n., 50.
Wesselofsky, A.: Ed. *Novella del Re di Dacia,* 69 n., 70 n.
Westermarck, Edward: *History of Human Marriage,* 43 n.; *Origin of the Moral Ideas,* 81 n.
Wilhelm, R.: *Chinesische Volksmärchen,* 20 n.
William, Count of Holland: 119.
Wimfeling, Jacob: 7, 99 and n., 104 n.
Winter's Tale, A: 61.
Witch as persecutor: 12, 15, 20, 26, 28, 62, 113.
Witchcraft, accusation of: 60, 63, 113.
Wolf, F.: *Über die neuesten Leistungen der Franzosen,* 95 n., 104 n.; *Über die Oliva-Saga,* 95 n.
Wolf, J. W.: *Niederländische Sagen,* 20 n., 81 n.
Wolfdietrich: 100 and n., 101, 102.
Worde, Wynkyn de: 84.
Wright, Thomas: Ed. of *The Canterbury Tales,* 132.

Yde et Olive: 69 n., 72, 78.
Ystoria Regis Franchorum: 69 n.

Zaunert, P.: *Deutsche Märchen seit Grimm,* 16 n., 50.
Zingerle, J.: *Kinder- und Hausmächen,* 27 n.